Envision To Profit FROM THE POWER OF MOBILE SOCIAL MEDIA IN SOCIAL CUSTOMER ENGAGEMENT

Learn Effective Mobile Optimized Strategies from the Best of both Chinese and Western Worlds to Grow Your Business

LAURA MAYA

PARTRIDGE
A Penguin Random House Company

To order additional copies of this book, contact
Toll Free 800 101 2657 (Singapore)
Toll Free 1 800 81 7340 (Malaysia)
orders.singapore@partridgepublishing.com

www.partridgepublishing.com/singapore

Knowing others is intelligence;

Knowing Yourself is True Wisdom.

Mastering Others is Strength;

Mastering Yourself is True Power

Lao Tzu

Introduction

The new digital media are rapidly becoming the easiest way for businesses and marketers to reach their audiences. Never before, have businesses had access to such a wide range of audiences, thanks to the new media of the "social web". Even with its increasing popularity, many businesses are still only beginning to adapt to and learning about the use of social media for their business. Most are still learning the ropes and are far from their maximum potential.

Today, both consumers and marketers are increasingly surfing information and connecting with each other through technological platforms. They blog, and they are quick to share their views, especially with easy access both through the desktop and from their mobile gadgets and smartphones. Mobile-enabled technology has brought on a mobility revolution, which, along with the social web, has brought forth a revolutionary transformation: *The Technological Convergence of Mobility and Social Networking*

This convergence occurs where one or more individuals of similar interests or commonalities converse using a social media platform with their mobile devices. As in web based social networking, mobile social networking occurs in virtual communities. Therefore, enterprises and marketers must find new strategies to engage with consumers on this platform. The requirement to remain innovative and ahead of the latest trends has increasingly encouraged brands to implement mobile applications and online platforms.

New technologies that are frequently being used by people to communicate, like SMS, tweeting, and micro blogging, while on the move will be of the utmost significance for enhancing a brand's interaction with consumers, especially when seeking to achieve "cool" technological effects for the user. Consumers are savvier nowadays, and they prefer to use interactive technologies that enhance their profile with friends and associates. Therefore, businesses need to understand the urgency of the need to adopt mobile initiatives and social networking to engage with consumers, as it will lead to improved sales and valuable customer feedback. However, one the decision to invest is made, the question remains: how can you find the perfect balance between engagement, social media, and mobility?

Statistics show how the Internet and the use of social media have grown over the years. Having a website has become a necessity for large corporations and small businesses alike, and it plays a major role in the social web. Now, most businesses and professionals have realized that the mobile social web is here to stay and that they need to be to be part of the system. This realization ensures a better chance of survival in the world of business.

Mobile social media is the new, mind-blowing wave in internet technology. It is an interactive conversational system that allows people to get together and socialize, learn, and/or advertise their business ideas or products all at the same time. You can directly converse with and get feedback from your audiences. People are more comfortable doing business with someone they can interact with instead of just a name on a screen or a static advertisement.

T his book explores different options for using the mobile social web to supplement your business development in business to consumer, consumer to consumer and business to business conversation.

This book will answer all your questions and introduce the fundamental marketing concepts needed to build an effective social media marketing strategy. These instructions will guide you through the knowledge of online marketing and use of mobile social media tools, clarifying "why" mobile social media is the strategy you should follow. Its goal is to provide several ways for businesses and professional to have a more effective online presence, from the local to the national, international, and global.

You will understand how to integrate mobile and social networking into your marketing plans. This is done by using the latest social media tools, like Quick Response (QR) code, mobile apps, location-based marketing, and others to increase your sales and revenue. This book also offers a firm understanding of which tools will suit your marketing purpose. Follow these guidelines to set up your own social strategies and explore the advantages that mobile social media can bring to your marketing efforts and to the development of your business.

- Learn which tools to use, where to find them, and how to engage profitable target markets with mobile marketing + social networking
- Set your level of commitment: this book will outline how to develop businesses for success in mobile + social media arenas.

- Discuss ROI, and characteristics of parallel mobile social media practice between the Western and Chinese social landscapes in order to identify their differences to tweak your marketing plan appropriately.

Contents

CHAPTER 1

What are Web 2 and Cloud Computing?

Leverage Your Business & Marketing Power Using the Latest Tools Available on the Internet!

The key to making your business successful is to use Web 2.0 with the aid of mobile social media sites. For those who are just beginning their online marketing or advertising journey, it is important to note that Web 2.0 and social media are one and the same. Social sites are an excellent way to get personal referrals by "word of mouth"; this works well with mobile technology, which is the rapidly emerging wave of the future.

Marketers and enterprises are encouraged to fully embrace the new technologies and to integrate them into your business—from your marketing, to how you interact with customers and staff, to how you manage your marketing and administrative tasks, etc.

This integration includes social media marketing with mobile marketing technology and taking advantage of all the benefits that today's technologies have to offer, including: webinars and other types of virtual events, social networking, mobile

1

apps technology, cloud computing . . . and any other type of technology that will help you increase productivity, efficiency, and profitability.

Enterprises that are late to embrace such technology will be left behind very quickly. The years 2012 to 2015 will be a major 'game-changing' period for how business is being conducted. Mobile social media technology in particular is having a significant impact on the way people live and the way how businesses are being conducted today.

People who are looking to buy products are more likely to buy from someone with whom they have interacted with instead of a complete stranger. Clients have more trust in people or entities that they know better. Whether they are buying online or in person, they feel more comfortable doing business with a name they recognize or have knowledge of. Times are changing, and the movement is on the internet.

Many, like you, may not be aware of the history of the Social Media era and how it came about. Most people who have been dealing online over the last decade or more have witnessed it: many were victims of (or have at least heard about) the "dot com bubble" bursting in the fall of 2001. Fortunes that had been made over the internet were all lost overnight, in the blink of an eye. The bubble was a passing fad that went away quickly, leaving many disillusioned, and some with empty pockets.

For some people, it seemed as though the sky was falling and the world was ending. One day, everything was fine and their business is steadily growing. However, the next day it was gone.

The World Wide Web was blamed for the fallout since many thought it was just a flash in the pan; many suspected that it had been an over-hyped scheme, but the crash was irrefutable proof.

There were survivors of the 2001 dot com burst, and these survivors had important things in common. Believers continued to insist that the World Wide Web was more important than ever and had a very bright future. These people hung in there; today, they are successful internet marketers.

One of those who saw the results of the 2001 dot com burst as a 'glass half full' rather than a 'glass half empty' was a man by the name of Tim O'Reilly. O'Reilly, of O'Reilly Media, met with Dale Dougherty of Media Live International in 2004.

Tim O'Reilly defines Web 2.0 as, "the business revolution in the computer industry caused by the move to the internet as a platform, and an attempt to understand the rules for success on that new platform."

There are many rules to follow if you wish to be successful online, but there is one important rule you must follow.

"You must build applications that harness network effects to build themselves larger and better as the usage by people increases."

Web 2.0 can be viewed as an upgrade to the World Wide Web. It is still the web, but a new, improved, and more interactive version. New technologies such as blogs, social bookmarking, wikis, podcasts, and RSS feeds are just some of the few that are shaping the direction of social media strategies. There are obvious differences between Web 1.0 (the web prior to the conception of Web 2.0) and Web 2.0. Some of these differences are:

- DoubleClick has been replaced by Google AdSense, as Google took over the company
- Britannica Online was replaced by Wikipedia—providing easy online access
- Personal Web Pages were replaced by Blogs
- Content Management Systems were replaced by Wikis
- Directories were replaced by Tagging, which simplifies search and categorization

These demonstrate the essence of Web 2.0. Instead of suffering the fate of the other Dot Coms, they thrived and survived through the downturn by applying the new principles of Web 2.0. Their success is so widely known precisely because they signify the changes in strategies and the embracing of Web 2.0 principles.

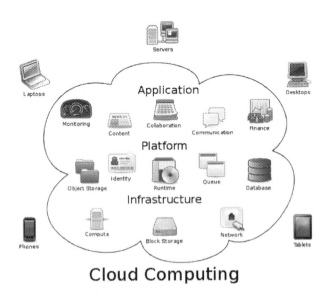

Cloud Computing

Web 1.0 was more about website building and the adaptation to the faster broadband speed in comparison to dial up ISPs. Software publishers and webhosting companieswere some of the earliest developers and major users of the Web 1.0 platform, testing their business strategies by introducing web hosting businesses for website site developers, helping companies more efficiently manage new online business processes.

If you look carefully, you will notice other differences between Web 1.0 and Web 2.0. Web 1.0 was driven and controlled by the "powers-that-be," while Web 2.0 is driven by users. This makes a huge difference. This power shift is making Web 2.0 more and more user friendly while making it more and more accessible and engaging for the average user.

The introduction of Web 2.0 has coincided with rapid adoption of broadband super-speed connections; the Internet has become much more than a huge online business website to make an online purchase. It has become a gathering place where social communities are formed, personal information is shared, and people converse and develop acquaintances. Community engagement has become one of the major mechanisms used in social networking platform to promote online gaming and commerce, and digital media products are becoming increasingly popular.

Today anybody with a new media idea, a few dollars, and just a little know-how, can build a successful Web 2.0 website that is completely interactive. All you need is an idea and the drive to succeed. While we are elaborating on Web 2.0, Web 3.0 is already out, though it is still in its infancy, with cloud computing also on the horizon, driving the emergence of Web 3. 0. The new advancement has seen great development in cloud computing, where social media sites usually make use of the cloud computing platform to support their activities, providing freeonline storage services. This enables users to tap into software and services stored in data centers rather than on a user's PC.

Web 3.0 users will experience easier accessibility of their acquired data through remote cloud sites via their mobile internet devices—users will be able to experience the Web on a phone, or move from device to device, instead of being limited to a PC. For this reason, the high speed broadband that supported Web 2.0 may not be enough to uphold the web infrastructure; Web 3.0 will be able to utilize the tools for both Web 1.0 and 2.0 and enable them to be used for mobile platform. Mobile tools like text messaging, tablet and smartphone applications, and geolocation are continually being enhanced with better features with Web 3.0.

Therefore, there are further developments set to happen before Web 3.0 becomes the new internet multiplatform paradigm.

For now, we will take a brief look at some of the upcoming trends and technologies and how Web 3.0 is going to change the landscape.

Today, you do not necessarily always need a Notebook in order to browse the Web. Web Browsers can be accessed almost everywhere—from gaming consoles (Wii and PS3), iPad Tablets, Android Smartphones, and even Smart televisions.

Web 3.0—also known as the semantic web or the meaning of data—represents a web were the context of content is defined by data. This refers to the web study of interlinked documents accessed via the Internet. Web pages are generally written in HTML, which describes the structure of information (i.e., the syntax) but not the semantics. However, if the computers can understand the meaning behind the information, this can provide an effective way to find the information that we are looking for. Web 3.0, in simple terms, means a web capable of reading and understanding content and context.

So, when a computer understands what data means, it can do intelligent analysis: this involves speculative reasoning and a combination of simple web searches to derive the result. Therefore, the web browser will become smarter as it is able to learn based on the information you search and share. Meanwhile, with more accessibility and flexibility in its infrastructure, it will be become more compatible with mobile technology.

If computers can understand and diagnose the meaning behind the semantic data, then they can speculate as to what we are interested in and can serve to help us better find what we want. This is really what Web 3.0—the semantic web—is all about.

Cloud computing

A major benefit to all web users of Web 3.0 is its ability to access data from anywhere through the cloud platform. This is mainly driven by the technological advancement in mobile-enabled devices like the iPad, smartphones, and cloud applications.

The main idea is to make sure that the users can access as much data as possible from anywhere, not just their home. This also includes Smart televisions, where social networking and search functions can also be done from your television through smart multimedia devices in the comfort of your living room.

Cloud Computing - in Simple Format

1) Cloud computing allow a computing model to access software ,server and storage resources over the internet

2) Netizen does not require to maintain and manage there resources on your own servers but is allowed to access and use them over the internet through a Web br~~~~

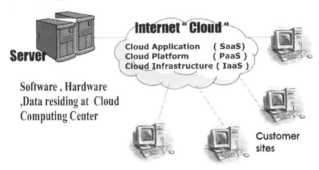

Server

Software , Hardware ,Data residing at Cloud Computing Center

Internet " Cloud "
Cloud Application   (SaaS)
Cloud Platform   (PaaS)
Cloud Infrastructure (IaaS)

Customer sites

Cloud computing (Putting it Simply)

Recently, there has been quite a lot of buzz about cloud computing. In this book, we will discuss the architecture of cloud computing in more detail in the final chapter. At this point, we will briefly explain how the technology works.

Cloud computing will permit users to access and utilize certain applications on any personal computer. These applications do not need to be installed on a laptop or computer. As long as the device has internet access, it can access the cloud.

The flexibility of accessing the cloud is that it does not require a specific laptop, computer, or location to access to data. In commercial terms, it is "Log-in on the Move," on-demand computing, where the user can access applications, computing resources, and services by the cloud's service provider via the Internet. Users are allowed to plug-in to the cloud for their infrastructure services, platform (operating system) services, or software services (such as software-as-service [SAAS] apps), treating the "cloud" much as they would an internal data center.

Some web hosting companies provide offers on cloud computing in the form of VPS hosting, shared Hosting (i.e., Exabyte) and SAAS. Common cloud services in the form of SaaS are those hosted by Microsoft Hosted Exchange and SharePoint.

For such a large scale setup, hosting companies will have thousands of servers located at data centers running tens of thousands of applications. When accessed by millions of users at the same time, each will be managed by a dedicated computing data center and self service capabilities in order to provide secure access to computing resources for various user roles, including cloud operators, cloud service providers, resellers, IT administrators, application users, etc.

Therefore, the future of e-Commerce, websites, web hosting, and data storage and its components are deeply intertwined with cloud computing.

For common netizens, cloud hosting is the latest technology to make use of the Internet to store applications, website files, data, etc. Liberating data from physical servers, this enables website owners and businesses to use the applications on their own websites. This includes a company's accounting system on any Internet-connected PC or laptop without installations, purchases of software licenses, or upgrade of hardware. A good example of cloud technology users is Gmail, which allows its multi-million users to always enjoy the fastest website loading speed, even in peak hours, by hosting its servers on a cloud platform.

An Illustrative Analogy for Cloud Computing/Hosting

Imagine you are a business owner who, from time to time, has business guests traveling from overseas on business trips.

Since you need the service of hotel accommodation for your guests so frequently:

Would your company consider buying or owning a hotel?

The answer is a resounding "NO" as you are not an hotelier—investing your time and money to learn about hotel management and building (or acquiring a hotel) is definitely not on your wish list.

So, why bother owning a hotel and having all the trouble of maintaining it if you can rent more rooms existing hotels.

Not only that, the hotel you rent may even offer a great number of add-on facilities or services, such as restaurants, business centers, conference rooms, spas, bars, etc., and you can choose to use them and pay for them only when you use the services, and not pay a single cent when you are not using them. Most importantly, the hotel and its in-house facilities are maintained by a group of industry experts and professionals.

As your business grows and your number of visiting guests increases, you are free to combine the services of a few hotels together, and use a few hundred rooms without any on-going obligation. And if one day you decide that you want to change your hotel, you can always do so as you are not tied up by agreement of any sort. However, if the hotel serves you well and you really like their services, you can always choose to stay.

The above concept is similar to using cloud computing services, though, of course, the flexibility and benefits are different for online applications. Some of these benefits include:

1. **Unlimited computing/website power whenever you need it**
    Cloud computing/hosting gives your websites unlimited computing power, such as bandwidth, RAM, CPU power, storage, etc. on demand whenever you need it.

2. **High availability and self-healing virtual machine**
    If your server hardware or virtual machine fails, your site will automatically be moved to other servers within the cloud and recovers in minutes.

3. **Best website experience**
    When you have unlimited computing/website power on demand, issues like website or server downtime and slow website loading speed during peak-hour traffic surges

are totally eliminated: superb website experience and performance are guaranteed.

4. **More internal IT resources and 24/7 reliable technical support**
   With cloud hosting, you are shifting the burden of your in-house IT team to your cloud hosting provider, to take care of all your server needs so that your team can focus on e-Commerce related tasks. Moreover, your virtual machines are supported by IT professionals standing by 24/7 to answer to your technical concerns.

The Applications of Cloud Computing/Hosting

Mobile and Social Networking Sites

For owners of mobile and social media sites on which members extensively share photos, videos, and music, the adoption of cloud hosting allows smooth surfing during traffic surge in peak hours, along with cost saving during off peak times.

Web Applications

For owners of e-Commerce sites that simultaneously run multiple web applications such as order status check, file sharing, and data storing, cloud hosting improves website loading speed without having to make expensive investmentsin hardware.

Facebook Applications

For program/gamedevelopers of Facebook, hosting their applications/games on cloud servers ensures the websites run at optimum speed even if visitors access/browse them from a remote location.

Business Applications

Owners of e-Commerce sites can avoid site overloading when multiple customers simultaneously place their orders, make payments and chat on live chat. With cloud hosting, e-Commerce site owners focus on their e-Business and profits instead of the hardware. There are many distinct kinds of cloud computing.

The first type that we will discuss is SaaS. It's cost effective and really simple for the company to use the "software as a service" application where it rents from or pay to use from a hosted platform for a specific kind of application. And the company does not actually do any development to any part of the software hosted there but except to configure some application setting only. The cloud providers will manage the infrastructure and platforms on which the applications run.

The next type of cloud computing is called utility computing. It is generally used by many corporations for requirements which are not so important. This kind of computing is normally a supplemental kind of computing for a firm who rent the technical infrastructure from the cloud provider to run their application such that they don't have to cost in owning expensive specific servers in replace the cloud providers contributes different options of computing resources which consist of virtual servers and storage as utility computing service.

The final type of cloud computing is Net services inside the cloud. This sort of computing is quite similar to the type of computing that is performed with SaaS. In this type of computing the World Wide Web is exploited for its functionality. Applications are genuinely delivered with this sort of computing through cloud server's hosted virtually

Cloud Providers will charge based on bandwidth usage or a monthly subscription fee for the use of their various cloud computing services

CHAPTER 2

Web 2.0 Social Media Makes Business Sense

Social media could not exist without the users and web surfers, who are all intertwined with the internet. They are real people who are using the social web, and who accept the development of an on-going relationship.

There is no immutable set of guidelines for social media marketing; in order to understand the trend, it is clearly important for each reader to be able to differentiate the definitions of social media and social media marketing.

Social Media is part of Web 2.0; it involves the process of online publishing and the application of communication tools sites for online conversation, engagement, and participation.

Social media marketing is another form of marketing, but one that uses Web 2.0 technology as its platform for direct or indirect marketing to build product and brand awareness, recognition, and business. Personal power marketing uses tools of the social web, such as social Networking, blogging, micro-blogging, social bookmarking and content sharing, which further facilitate online relationships and information sharing

Why the Time Is Now?

Many websites are now at the top of their game. They have plenty of power and alluring graphics, which entice customers and viewers of the web. Those who have just joined web marketing or launched their own websites may think that they are considered an 'old hat' and that those practices are falling far and far behind. However, that is not true! Newbies can easily catch up if they put the right tool to the right use.

We all know that people enjoy being able to interact on websites in more ways than one. With the technology currently available, the possibilities of creating such a site are only limited by your imagination.

All users of the web want to find answers easily, be entertained, and be efficient. Therefore, they expect websites to be interactive and user friendly. They should allow users to post queries whenever needed; they should provide helpdesks and relevant information about products and services. Sites that fail to provide such services quickly lose their attraction and do not deserve a second glance from the customers.

An average visitor of a website only stays for about 30 seconds at most. Therefore, successful websites must be able to grasp and hold their attention.

But how do you do this?

The internet is basically a platform for information, which customers and browsers go to to find what they want. So, providing relevant information that is straight to the point is necessary in gaining the viewer's attention. Do not beat about the bush before telling your customers what they want. They do not have the time to wait for answers. In order for you to sustain their attention, you should try including a forum for the customers to discuss; or even open a platform for feedback. Allowing customers to give feedback shows that you do treat them seriously. It does not just stop there. You should also act upon the feedbacks; otherwise, the feedbacks and forums will not be essentially pointless.

Innovations in the Web

Let's look at a few of the innovations of Web 2.0 and how these innovations have changed the way we use the World Wide Web. Social networking is not a new phenomenon: since long before Web 2.0 technology came into existence, people were already communicating through the internet on bulletin boards and forums. With discussion groups, they could log-on at any time to post and to read other members' posts. The exchanges and formats are quite convenient, and still offer the possibility of forming good bonds within fellow group members.

What are Social Networking Sites?

The basic idea of social networking is to have groups of people, usually with similar interests, come together for networking with others online. In order to make it exclusive to the members, they create nicknames with profiles and passwords. This creates an identity to signify that they belong to certain group/ organizations. Most of these sites focus on staying in touch with members; reconnecting with old/long-lost acquaintances or friends; making new contacts through discussions on topics like music and movies; or even wider scopes of subjects like hobbies, romance, finding dates, and job recommendations.

Sites like Facebook, MySpace, and Netlog are among the most popular sites for individuals, while there are also specific Social Networking sites that are tailored towards businesses or professionals. These networking sites will focus on exchanging information, career opportunities, business ventures, job consultancy service, expertise skills, business deals, promotional campaigns, and many others.

These sites include LinkedIn, Pinterest Ning, Ecademy, Xing, Viadeo, Ryze, Connects, network2connect, and many more. It started with the advent of instant messaging technology, but it has grown far beyond that.

In today's Web 2.0 world, both social networking and complete anonymity are possible. Online dating sites are very good examples of these two things operating in tandem. People can register and pay for membership to an online dating site where they may conduct an entire relationship for months without either party knowing personal information such as the other party's real name, ISP email address, or even the name of the city in which they live.

All communication is conducted through the online dating website itself, thus affording both social networking and anonymity. Only when both parties become comfortable with each other will they begin to share personal information.

Social Benefits of Social Networking Sites

Most social networking sites are not dedicated to a specific group. They are general membership sites, and the members themselves are divided into appropriate groups according to their interests and compatibility.

Most of the social networking sites are free to join. Once a profile is set up, you can start networking immediately. There are relatively few that require membership fees upon signing up. The site owners make their money from advertisements rather than from users. There are also sites that are open to members by invitation only. The latest examples are Google+ (plus) and Pinterest.

Besides making friends and networking online, the technological features provided by such sites are also useful. These features are only be available, as a package, when the user enrolls. Such features includes:

- Ability to target potential clients
- Broadcasting messages faster to your targeted customer.
- Photo-sharing with emailing function
- Blog-setup templates to incorporate micro-blogs within their networking site account

You can make posts to your blog and you can invite others to post to your blog. The trick here is to use the social bookmarking sites to their fullest potential. Upload links to your blog posts with appropriate tags, making sure they contain key words.

The blogs on social networking sites are in addition to (and not a replacement for) blogs created originally by you. If you are an internet marketer, the social bookmarking sites should be used to upload links to your blogs and website as part of your online strategy. This is a great way to enhance your online business and have fun in the process. You can meet some of your very best potential customers on social networking sites. You can also "make friends and influence people."

It is a well-established fact that more business is actually conducted in social settings than in an office: more deals are made on golf courses than in boardrooms.

More sales are made using social networking sites on the Internet than through all of the paid-for advertising combined.

People **HATE** commercials, but they are willing to listen to the recommendations that their friends have for a product or service. Not only do they not mind listening . . . they might go all out and seek more information on that product or service.

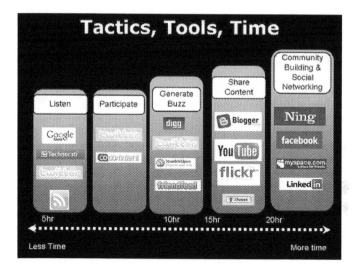

Social networking sites are great when used as a tool for research. In addition to being a great way to advertise, it is a rich market research resource that should not be overlooked. You can simply look through a social networking site and find out exactly what people are thinking about rather than conduct expensive and time-consuming surveys.

You can identify their problems and what measures they take to solve those problems. You can find out their interests and how they pursue them. By using social networking sites as a research tool, you can get better information and more of it in a single hour for free than you could get spending hours sending out surveys and trying to decipher the results.

Social networking is not simply a group of like-minded people exchanging information of mutual interests. If you tap into the system properly, it opens a multitude of possibilities: it offers more functionality, more members and friends, and opens up a more diversified range of audiences that can be reached 24/7, 365 days-a-year.

It is important when you are using social networking sites that you remember this and conduct yourself accordingly. If you join a site and start posting blatant advertisements, you are not using social networking properly and will probably get blocked by other users.

Simply advertising will get you nowhere. If you establish yourself as part of a group, then you become part of the social network.

Social networking is valuable but it can be made doubly valuable by using the content of the social networking sites in conjunction with social bookmarking intelligence. (The concept and understanding of how to use the social bookmarking techniques and content sharing procedure will be discussed at later stage of the book.)

Once you join a social networking website, find and build a group of friends online who are interested in the topic of your blog. It is helpful set reminders to frequently create posts and blog comments to your own blog on the social networking sites as well as to the blogs of others. While doing that, be certain to use the appropriate keywords in those tags to make them content-effective. This is so that the post can be easily searched and crawled by in the search engine's spider.

Combined together, these elements make an excellent marketing strategy. This is an effective way to help market your websites, blogs, products, and services. In addition, you get to enjoy what you're doing. Do keep in mind that it is important to grow your presence in order to increase your business. Therefore, maintaining profiles on multiple social networking sites is essential, as long as you selective choose the right sites (i.e., those that include your target audience).

You will meet people that you will like, become friends with, and even admire and respect. You should try not to create too many profiles by registering on too many sites, as it may cause you to be overstressed in maintaining your profiles. Stretching yourself too thinly may make it difficult to get the quality networking contacts you need.

CHAPTER 3

Blogging to Increase Your Visibility

The term blog was derived from the blending of the two words 'web' and 'log' creating the new term . . . blog. Early in the history of the World Wide Web, people could build personal web pages. These personal web pages were static websites, and only the owner of the website could post information about himself or his interests, while others could only read the information that was posted. The owner could keep an online journal that they could allow others to read, but it was a 'read only' site (i.e., not interactive).

Blogging software was developed, and it changed static personal journals into blogs that were interactive. Now those who had personal websites could not only post about themselves, but they could allow their visitors to comment on what had been posted or ask questions.

Blogs generate conversation whenever people visit. They could post on blogs all over the Internet about any and every subject imaginable.

Blogging and Micro Blogging

Blogging can be easily integrated as part of your social networking efforts.

As technology advances, building up websites started to become easier and easier. This led to more and more people building their own blogs. Blogging is more of a source to share information and a way to socialize, and it is the perfect platforms for busy professionals. Being dynamic, it encourages your audiences to interact with you. When they post a comment on your posts, they will get to know you better when you reply.

Conversations with visitors to your site will provide opportunities to establish your credibility and to build rapport. Thus, a network of friends can also be built-up overtime. This will help to increase the visibility of your product and service through your blog.

Blogs play a major role in Social Media. Likewise, it is the major and central foundation for all marketers who use Social media Marketing to sell their products. It is actually the main and central distribution hub where you can update your blog contents and distribute to your social networking sites (automated via the use of RSS) to keep your friends up-to-date. By using this method, you will keep your friends posted regularly and be fully engaged with them. This all contributes to enrichingthe social relationship between you and your readers. In addition, it helps to encourage your friends and audiences to visit your blogs frequently. With this, you would have established a certain level of credibility for your brand, products, or services, and aggregate all of your social media content.

A website's traffic is the main key to unlock successful internet marketing. We all know that. However, not many know that the secret of creating an astounding amount of traffic to a blog website can be achieved by using content sharing and Social Bookmarking methods.

These social bookmarking sites allow users to upload their favoriteslinks and store them on the site, and at the same time share them on the site's browser list. Others can view and click on these links to vote and comment on them. Users are able to categorize their lists and create tags for each individual link. Every time another user clicks on a link in a user's list, a back link is created. As the number back links multiply the indexing is then accelerated.

Another effective Web 2.0 creation is microblogging. This is the process of publishing short updates online (usually within the limit of 160 characters or less). Such tools include: Twitter, Weibo, identi, Yammer, Plurk, and QQzone (Chinese).

The popularity of these tools has been increasing and penetrating into China. Chinese bloggers have become increasingly aware of the effectiveness of Twitter and many other popular social bookmarking sites (like addthis.com). This has caused the creation of similar sites in the Chinese language—this trend (which we saw earlier) is applicable to those who wish to penetrate into the China market and introduce their products and services.

When a blog is created by a user, there are many choices that must be made. The first and most obvious choice is the topic of the blog. For those who plan to monetize their blog, the choice of topic is a crucial one. It will make the difference between success and failure.

If a user is already an active internet marketer and has a particular niche, it makes the choice easier. However, if the user has only just begun internet marketing, choosing the topic can be a lot more difficult.

Keyword research is highly necessary. One of the best ways to research and find a viable topic is by visiting other blog sites and forum sites on the Internet. Finding the right niche will help your blog to become exclusive. This will be excellent for those who know how to look for strong keywords and will then be able to provide a good ranking for your blog.

The following will set the stage for you. By using the various steps below, you will be able to plan and produce a strong, effective blog. If you have started up a blog, review the list to make sure that it is on track and ready to be integrated it with your social media goals.

Steps to Increase you blog's visibility and credibility:

- Brand building—reinforce your brand
- Building community—similar interest groups
- Educate, Entertain, Engage and Enrich—address specific interest to ensure a wholesome engagement
- Be open to new opportunities and find new prospects
- Self-publishing of high quality content
- Sales &marketing—broadcasting with webcasting and podcasting tools
- Use a forum for customers' feedback and after sales services (if applicable)

Once you have selected a topic, the next step is to actually build a blog.

There are many web-hosting companies, and many of them offer blogging services. There are even web-hosting companies that specialize in blogging websites. One of the better known companies is Word Press, but there are many others out there. In order to help market a business, you may wish to hire a social media manager to set up your social media marketing strategy and your blog for you.

There was a time when only gurus could build websites. It was necessary to be proficient in the use of HTML, among many other things—but that is no longer the case. Web 2.0 technology allows even novices who have never thought of building their own website to not only build one but to also do it very quickly and efficiently.

There are some things that you may have to know before building a blog. Fret not: there are blog websites that can teach you how to build a blog website, or you could join a group on your favorite social networking site and ask questions about it. Resources are readily available almost everywhere. That's the great part of Web 2.0! Everything you need to know can be found online, including people to help you learn.

These opportunities are opened to people from all walks of life, to pursue this interest. Senior management of businesses who joined the computer era at a later stage can also easily catch up to the younger net savvies, to explore the world of the social web as well.

New Mobile Blogging on the Go

Once a blog website is up and running, it is important to get the search engine spiders to visit the site so it can be indexed. Once the site is indexed, it will appear in searches made on search engine sites

As blogs are mainly user-driven, the owner of the blog has control of its content. He may also allow visitors to his blog website to add content, and some even allow content to be edited by users. This feature was the main factor that made interactive blogs popular. Audiences are no longer just observers on the sideline; they get to participate in the games as well. They are now a part of the game.

Many novice blog builders use RSS feeds, podcasts, and webcasts to enhance their blog websites. Some people simply read the posts, but many people like to be more interactive. People like to get information via audio, video, or sharing of pictures. By using these mediums, the blog owner is able to hold a visitor's attention longer.

Mobile blogging has emerged as a further savvy communication platform for bloggers who want to update their readers while on the go. Any mobile blogger with an Internet-capable cell phone can utilize this method to update their blogs regularly. A mobile blog photo can be taken with a camera phone and then uploaded to the user's blog via their mobile browser. Inclusion of caption heading and comments are features made readily available. Likewise, a BlogSpot with a short article can be posted from a smart phone at anytime and anywhere.

You can find very active blogs that discuss controversial topics like politics and religion. You can also find blogs that are dedicated to nothing more than pure pleasure. These sites might include topics such as travel, gardening, fishing, book reviews, cooking recipes, sewing, boating, etc.

Find a topic that you are interested in or even passionate about. Go out there and start your own blog. Construct the site well, pursue social bookmarking, and you can begin to create your own online empire.

If you find that you need some assistance, find a social media manager to do the legwork for you. This is to ensure that you can get started without the hassle of learning how to do it on your own. However, you may want to decide to pursue Social Media Marketing. It is your own personal or business choice, but the most important thing is to . . . *Get started now!*

Build Your Website with a Blog to be both Social- and Mobile-Friendly

Your Blog is your home base. It is also the core of your Mobile and Social media hub for your online business. It is where you drive people from your Social Networking sites to your mobile marketing apps. It is your main archive center, where most of your visitors can get information concerning your product and services.

Google has recently launched its Go Mobile (GoMo) initiative to encourage businesses to go mobile. Google has provided the marketers with tools and resources to make their websites more mobile friendly.

Website developers will be able to monitor how their sites look and perform while on mobile internet enabled devices. A support element with recommendations will be provided to help those developing more mobile friendly sites. The GoMo website recommends several selected partners for building mobile sites, such as iLoop, NetBiscuits, and Wapple. Other sites which are included are Atimio, DudaMobile, Google Site Builder, iLoop Mobile, Kishkee, Mobify, Moovweb, Unbound Commerce, Wix. com, and July systems.

For any marketers who wish to start the conversation and to present and showcase themselves as a leader in their field or an expert on a particular topic, the blog should serve as the major central hub for the venture.

Blog visitors can join the conversation by submitting comments on posts and voting for them. You will have to pay attention to the visitors' feedback and comments and help the marketers to build better relationships with potential customers.

Work on the concept of using your social networking site as your sub-blog station, where you make connections. Your blog or website can be treated as your main distribution hub. From here on, building good contents into your blog and establishing credibility for your brand and services, educating your prospects, and aggregating all your social media content will all be done from this hub.

Starting one is quick and easy, though, as we have warned all marketers before, maintaining a blog and keeping its content fresh, good, and interesting takes a serious amount of time and commitment.

The various steps outlined here are designed to get you up and running with a blog within a day or two. While building the blog, you need to have the pre-agenda plan in mind so that your blog will be built with a clear definition of how it works as the main hub links to your social media program.

Focus on the following main consideration when setting the stage:

- What are the business objective and goals you have for your blog
- How to use it to target your preferred readers
- How do you get your readers to opt-in, and use it for lead generation, incorporate RSS feeds, and add-on FeedBlitz
- Use the Blog as a Tool for creating sales and to help market your products and services.
- Consider a forum to provide a form of customer service by responding to feedback
- Use ShareThis, AddThis, and TweetThis—these are plug-ins for content sharing and bookmarking—making sure to do proper tagging and to ping them
- Mobile marketing is part of the agenda: build your website and blog to be mobile-friendly and compatible with the mobile web
- Incorporate the Google Analytics Plug-in: this provides measurement results with tracking capabilities for popular keywords, visitors' behavior, campaign results, etc.
- Search engine optimization is an important part of building a blog if you want search engines to put it up on a good ranking
- Choose nice color schemes, easy to use navigation templates (which are fast loading) and secure features to ensure your blog will be attractive, search engine friendly, and easily manageable

Once you have decided on the blogging application, follow the following quick-start plan to setup your blog:

Step 1: Blog Hosting service

There are many web hosts that provide easy-to-setup blogs with their very own content management systems. The CMS will allow you to make changes quickly and will give access to integrate dynamic data. Some examples of web publishing tools are, Wordpress, Drupal, Joomla, siteworkspro, mamboserver, etc.

You can select from a list of hosted options, using software such as Blogger's, typepad, Vox, or WordPress. If you decide to go on the non-hosted service, some of the popular domain registers are www.hostgator.com, www.dreamhost.com, www.register. com, and www.godaddy.com. On any of these sites, you can type in your preferred Domain name (which you have chosen) for your blog and see if the name is available for registration.

Step 2: Choose a Domain Name

Try to find a unique name for your blog. You can use keywords that are related to your business; also, due to recent developments, you can also choose any extensions other than .com. The new system allows companies and groups to apply for their own suffixes, which could be anything from a brand like ".Smartdevice" to something more broad, like ".XXX.description". Names will also be allowed in native scripts such as Arabic and Chinese.

Before deciding on your own blog name, test its uniqueness and research on how often is the word being searched by search engine, or do a simple search study on "GoogleTrend" Whatever name you choose, do not rush into a name you might end up to being unhappy with. Write a List and slowly narrow it down to the final choice.

Step 3: Choose a Blog Application

Your blogging software or platform is the technology that runs your blog. Hosted services like Blogger, Movabletype, and Wordpress provide ideal applications for people who are not computer gurus.

Non-hosted services, on the other hand, offer more complete control over your site, more flexibility, and more design options (examples are given as well). A larger company would probably want to host its own site on its own server for confidentiality purposes. For mobile blogging options, the following four sites are the pioneers in blog setups.

Google Mobile Blogger

This is one of the most accommodating blogging services that provide the most basic cell phone feature of updating blogs on the go. Blogger allows a mobile blogger to add posts via email or even SMS. To get started, you will need to register with Blogger. After receiving a designated code, the mobile blogger will have access to a mobile blog, or they can link the account to another blog. SMS users follow the same steps. Instead of sending an email message, they send a text with the word "register" to a specific account.

Bloggers who have an existing account and wish to merge their site can visit http://www.google.com/support/blogger for more details on the procedure.

WordPress Mobile

Though WordPress is a popular blogging service, the WordPress Laptop and Mobile Edition content management system allows consumers to edit, publish, and upload blogs from mobile devices. WordPress can be customized for the advanced mobile browsers. There is already a function within WordPress for updating a standard blog by email via the 'writing module' under settings. For easier blog set-up, they have provided blogging plug-in modules like:

- BlogPress (for iphone)
- WpTo Go Apps (for Android) Alexking.org/projects/ WordPress

WordPress Mobile Pack is a set of apps that allow blog administrators to edit posts from their mobile phones and make the blog more mobile-friendly for readers who wish to access their blog on-the-go.

Typepad

You can choose from a number of templates as well. With this software, updating a blog is as simple as sending an email. Images, audio, video, and links may be added to the blogs easily. For mobile application, the blogs may be updated from any location. Ideas, passions, opinions, and expertise may be shared through blogs. The tools on TypePad will help bloggers get their content recognized on social networking sites and also on search engines.

There are other developments like Posterous, Tumblr, Xanco, and Livejournal, each of whom provides Moblogging (mobile Blogging). For a more detailed list, please look up for the full list at the following link: http://mashable.com/2007/08/06/free-blog-hosts/

Mofuse Premium

This is a Paid-version of MoFuse for Blog, which enables mobile-site building and hosting services called MoFuse premium (Mofusepremium.com). It is powerful and fun to use. The sites it builds are quite nice, and it is very easy to turn a blog into a functional mobile site with this tool. (Further Tips are available on Mobile blogsetup)

Step 4: Remember Content is King

Good content will bring a great number of readers. The success of your business blog depends on the content. If you want visitors to visit frequently, the content of your blog needs to be frequently updated. It is central to blogging that the blogger writes or creates content that is attractive to readers.

You will need to customize your site to the needs of the audience. With due consideration of your goals, objectives, and your personal branding, you will be able to drive your blog's content quality through the roof. Any mobile marketing project should initially be designed with your target audience in mind—that is, your customers' needs! The simple truth is that your content must carry substance to ensure its success. Here, we have a suggested list of ideas that you may or may not use when writing the content. Enhancing the site for business, sharing, social bookmarking, and mobile friendliness should considered throughout.

List of possible ideas:

- Product Introduction with video demonstration
- Interview and testimonial from customers
- Promotions, product reviews, and market news
- QR code for mobile marketing and scanning
- Mobile application (App) description
- Industry events preview and review
- Photo of products or employees
- Trend analysis and promotion campaign

Other than the above list, some individuals who are blogging for their personal interests, can consider to blog on more specific subjects like, travelling, gadgets, food recipes, weight loss methods, books . . . the list goes on.

Good content can come in the form of very short posts. It can even be just a question to draw comments. Shorter posts are usually within the limit of 200 words.

A common example quoted will be for some videos on your site that requires the Flash program to activate or run. However, not all tablet devices are Flash video-compatible. Viewing the video may require the visitor to download a special application in order for their device to use the Flash program. You may therefore post a link in relation to the application on your site. This is so that users of smart mobile devices, like the iPhone, can immediately click to install it and view your videos without having to search for the application by themselves.

Traditional Advertising versus Social Media + Mobile Marketing

Posters, advertisements on the television, and radio are slowly receding in importance. They have not become obsolete, but such traditional media for advertising come with an overwhelming cost. These make the starting up of a business financially unbearable to many. Even so, traditional advertising—like billboards along the highways, newspapers, or even organizing a radio show—have still been very frequently used due to their effectiveness. However, the affordability issue is a problem for new startups and smaller companies.

Nevertheless, the development of Social Media and Mobile Marketing offer an affordable alternative. Standard advertising is rapidly losing its popularity due to Online advertisements. The latter are becoming more targetable and easier to use. With the new technology in place and on the internet, cell phones, and television, businesses are still using standard advertising. Those that have yet to use social media are finding themselves being left behind. Both methods of advertising do have their strengths, and capitalizing on these depend on the marketer's capability to combine both traditional and social media marketing. They will need help with funding and support. Once they are able to do so, they will be able to achieve full media domination.

When funded by a major corporation, both can be used for a new product launch or when they have a large budgetaimed at dominating competitors.

Social media and mobile marketing has opened an entire new world of advertising for businesses. Static sites used to advertise a business's services or products hold little interest for the average online visitor today.

People want websites to be more interactive and dynamic. Mobile friendly sites fulfill this need, as they can be engaged on the go and always switched on, accessing content at the touch of button—anytime, anywhere. At the very least, businesses want to be able to enquire whenever there have queries and respond quickly and appropriately. Visitors want to be able to read reviews on the products that they are searching for. They would usually look at forums for recommendations and comments. They would also see how customer's feedbacks are being dealt with before deciding to make their purchases.

Internet users today are very visual and enjoy watching videos, including those that entertain them but also those that provide knowledge they did not possess before coming to the site. Visuals or audios on the site may hold visitors attention and keep them on the website or mobile site

Videos are also a great way to advertise, not just on your website, but they can also be posted on other sites such as YouTube. Each time the video is viewed, it will have the potential to bring more traffic to your site. You also can increase your page ranking using videos.

Mobile and Social media sites are a great place to advertise, both directly and indirectly. By socializing on the social media sites, you (or your social media manager) can become 'friends' with others that share the same interests. During these chats, you may share links to stories, articles, reports, videos, or products on your website. Remember! People prefer to buy from people they consider as friends rather than a complete stranger.

Some social media sites, such as Facebook, also have ad-space available on their sites. Their advertising helps marketers to target keywords/interests. The demographic in which it is able to reach out to would be much better and more targeted by interests, as well as other demographic factors such as age group, gender, education, location, etc., instead of targeting users based on search intent and bidding on keywords. These ads have proven to be more effective and profitable than Google ads. This is because they are targeting based on groups with similar interests. These ads usually are cheaper and produce better results and higher sales than other ads.

Due to the advances in mobile technology, most people will look for local businesses online to get the phone number or address, instead of using the phone book and flipping through its pages. Once they find an address, they may even locate it using the GPS (Global Positioning System) in their phone. This eliminates the need to call and ask for directions.

CHAPTER 4

Mobile and Social Media: New Engagement

As 3G mobile broadband services progresses rapidly, the mobile application industry has witnessed a strong and rapid growth since 2008, bringing in higher levels of revenue through the mobile platform.

The rush for owning smartphones and the desire for creating more applications or mobile apps, has led to an explosion of the market in the Appstore business. This has helped to increase the price of its products and increasing the revenue earned. The mobile application industry took hold of the progressive growth in social network societies and started to merge and develop mobile social network applications with social networking sites

Examples of social network powerhouses are Facebook, Twitter, Linkedin, Myspace, and Weibo. They are already well known on the web and throughout the world. Some have already built new mobile platforms for new Social Networking Services (SNS).

This has helped bring about applications for many new social networks that allow mobile users to be able to participate. It is a platform where they can surf on mobile friendly sites and use the new geolocation features as a way to enhance their social network capabilities. People who are on the move are sometime too busy to just sit in front of their desktop computers to access their social media accounts. With internet-enabled cellphones, users can access their social media platforms via their phones. A study recently done by an analyst confirms that Facebook has seen a drastic jump in the number of users (from 20 million to 60 million visitors per month) coming from mobile phones. The use of social media and the number of cellphones owned is growing at dizzyingly high rate.

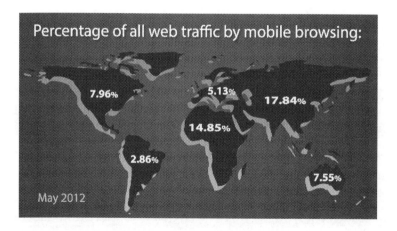

Around the world, there are more than 3 billion cell phone users—and more than 1,000 new customers are added every minute (as of July, 2008). China has 480 million cell-phone users, accounting for 35% of its population. In comparison, the United States has 230 million cell-phone users, representing 76% of its population (as of 2010).

Envision To Profit from the Power of Mobile Social Media
in Social Customer Engagement

The forecast for average annual growth in mobile-phone penetration rates in Asia from 2005 to 2010 ranges from 80.1% in India, 38.5% in Pakistan, 21.9% in China, 19.5% in Indonesia and 16.9% in the Philippines to 5.8% in Malaysia, 4.2% in Japan, 2.1% in Korea—and 4% in Singapore. (Stats report: Business Analytic International)

Globally, around 50 % of people use mobile devices, and the amount of mobile with access to internet is growing. Once the figures exceed 70%, every marketer will be forced to consider mobile marketing as part of their social media program.

Currently, text messaging, like SMS, and phone calls remain the most popular forms of social networking;these markets have generated over US 50 Billion in revenues for cell phone companies worldwide. By interacting with social media apps on one's phone, they work together to give an individual full access purchasing power at any given time;Revenue is expected to exceed one trillion all revenue gain through social media and mobile media technology.

A marketer just has to place a link to a product introduction blog on his social networking site or Facebook business page, then people can read the pageview from a smartphone and decide to click through to browse the product specification and promotional campaign, hopefully resulting in a sale. This shows a simple example of mobile social media marketing integration, as it appeals to the reader who is on his mobile device browsing to the marketer's blog or fanpage. In actual fact, mobile marketing and social media marketing are synergistic, each facilitating the other to generate interested traffic on relevant sites.

Another common method of text advertising, popularized in early 2004, is when a retailer text messages advertisements to prospective customers who have requested and opt-in to receive them. The retailer acknowledges the prospect with a special keyword to text to a number, much like a telephone number. When they do so, they receive a text message back asking them to confirm that they wish to subscribe. Then, when you wish to send a promotion out to your customers, you can do so.

For example, if you are a flower shop owner and are overstocked, you can instantly text your frequent loyalcustomers the message that anyone who buys flowers within a specified promotion window will get a free mobile coupon for a 50% discount on valentine day. Before you know it, you may find people calling up to place orders.

Such Mobile coupons have a redemption rate of 25% to 40%, which is more effective compared to the traditional print or mail coupons.

The main reason for this is that mobile marketing usually requires an opt-in, meaning that customers can choose to subscribe to your company's or campaign's messages in order to participate in the program. This means it is usuallyless intrusive than other methods of advertising.

With text messaging usage remains dominant and continues to grow, it is still consider the best way for customers to opt-in to a marketing program or for retailers to influence timely behavior through their marketing program. It will still be the most popular form of mobile marketing.

Easy Integration

The best thing about social media sites is that most of them are automatically optimized for mobile phone screens. Applications for mobile phones also play an important role in social media marketing. It is where a business keeps in touch with its customers via their mobile phones.

A business could easily have a presence on the mobile Web through its Facebook pages, foursquare venues, Ning or Twitter accounts, and other social network services. This can be done without having to spend money on site design or valuable time on testing a mobile-optimized company website.

Mobile access to social networks is on the rise. Marketers everywhere are looking for ways to combine these two powerful technologies. Recent cases include a few new location-based social networking sites likethe Socialight, Twingr, HelloTxt, and Shoutem. These sites are offering platforms that allow anyone to design, develop, and launch their very own social networks for mobile devices for friends or a community.

The tools they offer are perfect for designing a niche site for a selected group of users, and they provide location-based tagging features. This would allow companies to direct potential business for any products or brands. The social environment is tailored to the customers' specific needs, and this networking process can be linked to your Mobile Marketing website.

First and foremost, you need to set up a mobile website. This can be combined or converted into your existing websites. Many companies have automated systems that will transform your existing website information and reformat it to fit a mobile device. There are also plug-and-play options offered online that create a specific mobile website in addition to your regular website. Nevertheless, it is important that you do your research and find the best option out there for your company.

Next, you will need to register your business on a location-based platform like Facebook Places. This is like putting an advertisement on the Yellow Pages. If no one knows you're out there, you will not get much business. Once registered, you can totally immerse yourself in mobile marketing and start running your promotions.

In addition, you will never fully understand mobile marketing unless you use a mobile marketing technique to promote your business for trial—you will need to feel it first-hand. You should begin by playing with your internet-enabled tablets or smartphones and check out the various businesses in your local area, then take advantage of their mobile offers. Become familiar with all the extra features that your tablet and smartphone comes with. A couple of interesting features which you can look at are, QR code recognition features and purchasing apps online. The more you use your mobile device, the easier it becomes to understand mobile marketing.

ON LOCATION

2D BARCODES

You may want to try out your newfound marketing niche by running a mobile campaign. These can be purchased by your company on a cost per click basis. It's not all that difficult to setup these campaigns; all you need to do is visit some advertising websites and they'll walk you through step-by-step and help you setup your very first campaign

Lastly, you can utilize the QR codes (Quick Response Codes). These are two-dimensional matrix codes that you can scan or read with your iPhone, Android, or other camera-enabled Smartphone. By using the code, you can link digital contents on the web; activate a number of phone functions including email, Instant Messaging (IM), and SMS; connect the mobile device to a web browser or a specific mobile page that offers coupons; and add special offers and additional content; or it can be used for installing APPs.

Further, mobile phones enable people to easily "Like" you on Facebook or follow you on Twitter. This process is Immediate.

Cost-effectiveness

In comparison to the cost for establishing a mobile site for your business, enrolling to mobile advertising services, or even running a SMS campaign, marketers will still find social media campaign to be relatively lower in cost.

Profiles on various social media platforms are free for you to create. The maintenance or updates are relatively cheap or free. Furthermore, social media platforms make it easier to launch your own campaigns.

All in all, mobile marketing is not at all that difficult to set up. It is like any other forms of social media marketing except that the content is delivered through a mobile device.

The future of advertising is on the internet. It will soon be in higher demand than standard advertising. Not only will it be faster, it will also be more efficient, and more user-friendly; and **the best part of it is that most of it comes free!**

Social Media Marketing integrates well with Mobile marketing

Following the weekend riots in Tottenham and at various locations in London on August 2011, and the Major Iranian Presidential Election protest on June 2009, local authorities were quick to mention that the rioters had coordinated using the social web. They utilized the "social media" for fuelling the unrest.

From these instances and other, it has become obvious that communications are not happening only on social networking sites like, Facebook and Twitter. The handy mobile phone was the choice tool for communication for the young, urban rioters.

Both mediums play a major role in the spread of the news. People took to the social web and broadcasted their messages to friends through the internet, while those with mobile phones were sending text message and sharing photos (captured with their phones) online.

Again, the power of the social web and mobile web has proven its ability to push communication and engagement to spread information to targeted audiences. Even in its infancy, it has managed to display its might in crossing all borders and influencing the World. It also shows that both social media and mobile communication will need to integrate in the new era of mobile social media.

Change of Marketing Concept

In the earlier days, the general content of a course on marketing would have covered the four major points:

- Product
- Pricing
- Placement
- Promotion

Today, in social media terms, the four major points are still critical; however, they are infused with an additional four major points:

- Content
- Context
- Connection
- Community

The rule of marketing is changing as the infusion of all the eight major points begins. Social media marketing needs to widen its scope, and soon it will evolve into mobile media marketing. As cloud computing advances, its progresses will also be integrated into the system.

Today, social media and mobile media are intimately connected. It is almost impossible to go anywhere today—whether to work, to the airport, to a restaurant, shopping mall, or any other event or place—without seeing someone on a mobile device, or carrying one around.

Most social media platforms have a mobile application integrated in their source platform. Location-based social networking sites like Foursquare, Citysense, iPling, Loopt, Brightkite, and even Facebook specifically tailored their site with similar functions to cater to mobile phone users. This is so that both featured and smartphone users can share their locations through their GPS, mobile email, or SMS.

Smartphones in the Mobile Media Landscape

The evolution of mobile technologies of smartphones, combined with the desire to interact and acquire new and faster information on the social web, while on the go, makes it clear that mobile, location-based advertising is here to stay.

Smartphones are the latest form of mobile phone, with advanced computing abilities. They are able to access the internet through mobile internet browsers, and they are able to send and receive emails. They come with a built-in camera and are able to operate many applications.

According to a study by comscore, in 2010 100 million people in the world owned a smartphone. Another 50 million owned some other type of mobile device, like tablets.

We have seen an explosion in the use of mobile devices since 2008. We have also witnessed the emerging dominance of laptop

PCs over desktop PCs, with the tablet now rising in popularity. Simultaneously, we have seen changes from featured phones to smartphones.

With millions of smartphones in the world, their advent has influenced and redefined the methods that businesses and marketers will be using to promote their products and services. This has caused a rush for marketers to adopt the Social Media + Mobile Marketing platform.

Mobile marketing gives marketers the opportunity to reach out to their targeted customersdirectly. The questions on every marketers mind right now are, *what does the future hold?* And *What is in store for mobile marketing?*

Given the rapid developments in mobile technology, we can only expect mobile marketing to reach its zenith in the future. With the integration of more effective and greater functions generated from mediums like apps, a productivity tool which allows the device to perform specific tasks, customers will start to be more attracted to the digital media and its advertising methods. Smartphone users are exposed to a more flexible, personalized platform, equipped with more features that can help create better-looking graphics and more impressive videos.

Some of the mobile marketing methods include:

Mobile Web Advertising—Advertisements are placed on mobile websites as banner ads or as pay per-click ads. These can also be found on the mobile versions of search engines as sponsored ads.

Mobile Promotional Circulars—Digital Mobile circular promotional newsletters sent to the customers' phones directly.

Mobile In-appAdvertising—Admob, an advertising company owned by Google, provides an extension for developers to integrate advertisements into their Mobile Applications. Consumers can download them onto their phones from the appstores associated with their phones.

Location-Based Marketing—location-based advertising has taken the mobile medium by storm. This method has the ability to tie mobile vouchers, coupons, and promotions into a consumer's real-time location. Location-based advertising involves identifying the consumers' current position via the geopositioning on a mobile device.

Mobile Interactive Brand Marketing—This is a way of engaging customers through the mobile platform and enabling social interactivity and voting via mobile sites. An example of such an app would be a fashion magazine offering its customers the opportunity to vote and comment on its collection. The featured collections have interactive icons, allowing people to vote. This method can also encourage smartphone users to opt-in to their brand or product by offering appropriate mobile incentives.

Mobile Applications (Apps)—These are software programs that can be downloaded on a phone. These applications can be for entertainment or serve a useful function—there is a wide range of applications available for different purposes. Businesses can build their own apps or they can advertise on other people's apps. Such apps include, social networking apps, rich media content, games, or "viral" content.

Text messaging (SMS)—This is probably one of the most common forms of mobile marketing, as discussed in detail above.

Text messages are no longer than 160 characters each. They are sent directly to a person's phone through the cell phone carrier.

Increase in M-commerce

With mobile marketing rapidly becoming common, mobile shopping sales exceeded 2.6 billion in 2011. Purchasing transactions on the mobile platform with smartphones are becoming increasingly common. Marketers and online retailers are bound to capitalize on this trend and expand their promotion, marketing campaigns and sales using M-commerce. *So what are you waiting for?*

You can use M-commerce as part of your marketing strategy and a way to interact with potential customers on the move. In implementing M-commerce, you will need a prompt mobile internet presence offering a quick, easy, and engaging shopping experience for consumers.

Establishing your Niche/Brand using Social Media and Mobile Marketing

Your Niche/Business

You may already have a business you want to promote through Mobile and social media marketing; or maybe you have none and would like to give it a try. Maybe the idea of having a business on the internet that you can monitor or control via a laptop or Smartphone is appealing to you.

Ahhhhh . . . you do not have a business and you are not sure what you would like to try. It is not as hard as you might think to find a niche or a business to start up, and then make it successful. There are a few basic rules to follow to get started:

- Research the trends or topics that people are frequently searching for.
- Check the favorites of social media sites.
- Check the searches on the social bookmarking sites.
- Check both mobile and web-based search engines for top searches.

You should make a list of your core interest or core skills—things that you are skillful with, things that you enjoy to do, things that you are good at, things that you are knowledgeable about.

Compare the topics found in your research with your list. Check if there are any similarities in the topics. If so, you can start doing your own searches to see how popular the topic is and how much competition there is out there.

A good marketer makes just about anything to work, but success will depend on how much work you put into it and how much interest there is in the topic. Creating several small websites, about different topics, may work out better for you than having one larger website. One-page websites about a specific topic can be quite successful;these can include links to affiliated marketing products.

You may prefer to develop a more complicated website with multiple pages and multiple products. These may be successful if handled correctly, and if you are able to get the visitors attention and keep them on the site. However, you should always remember that it is easier to make a website successful if you limit the choices or decisions the user has to make. Simply interpreted, it means that you give the user one direction to follow and one door to go through. If they go through the door, they are more likely to make a purchase. Given too many choices, they may decide to think it over and come back later (which they probably would not do).

Do your homework. Pick a topic you can enjoy or are knowledgeable about, and make sure there is interest for it out there. If you follow these few guidelines, build your site correctly, and work it properly, you will be successful in your online business.

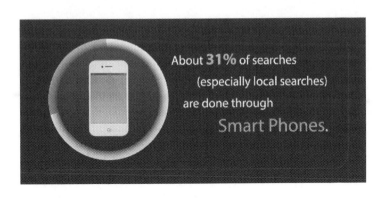

About **31%** of searches (especially local searches) are done through Smart Phones.

CHAPTER 5

Integrating Mobile Initiatives into your Marketing Strategies

Social media was established much earlier in a similar arena, where more and more conversations are taking place between customers and brands, friends, and business colleagues. More importantly, consumers are increasingly accessing their social media accounts from mobile devices everyday. This synergy with social mobile marketing services can help your business capitalize on this trend. It can help bridge the social media communication gap by using the mobile web.

With the emergence of smartphone technology, the concept of mobile social networking on the mobile web is being revolutionized. It became much easier with newer tools like the Facebook App, which allows mobile phone users to easily access the internet and get connected with their friends on the social networking sites.

According to Comscore, a US-Based analyst company, 31 percent of US smartphone users accessed social networking sites via their mobile devices over a period of three months ending in

January 2010. This is in comparison with just less than 7 percent of standard featured phones over the same period.

In China, analysts predict that the number of mobile social network users will reach 330 million by the end of 2012, using social networking sites like RenRen and Weibo. In the US, it is predicted that 110 million users occupy 65 percent of mobile internet users with mobile 3 G penetration

Therefore, it is important to integrate mobile initiatives into your marketing strategies. Also, understanding how social media and mobile technologies affect our potential customers and business colleagues.

Furthermore, these technologies can complement one another. With the value of social media and mobile media combined, a more successful campaign than when they are being used individually is possible. Here are a few key steps designed to optimize the power of integrated digital campaigns. This includes both mobile and social elements:

- **Ensure that your contents are easily accessible to multiple social media sites**

  Design and execute digital contents. Produce them to be mobile and easily accessible by all mainstream mobile devices and to be used by multiple social media platforms on smartphone devices such as BlackBerrys, Symbian, iPhones, and Android phones.

- ## Share your blog posts and e-newsletters

  Share your content through social media sites and your community sites, wherever and whenever possible. If customers receive emails via smartphone devices, they can immediately forward, share, and post your content with their own social networks. This will help to increase word-of-mouth marketing.

- ## Encourage the use of QR codes

  QR codes can be printed as a sticker to be placed on a door, to tag a specific location or an address. With a smartphone, you can snap and scan the codes to access more information related to the address directly online.

  This code can also be inserted into newsfeeds of the social networking sites. For marketers, QR codes provide an easy solution for linking offline contents from physical locations to online contents.

- ## Consider an app

  Building an application is a proven way to reach to consumers in a compelling way. This could be used for delivering company news, coupons, special discounts, or engaging customers around your social networking sites in campaigns like quizzes, polls, games, etc.

• Social location marketing

Location-based advertising and marketing campaigns usually allow an advertiser to send a message to a phone based on its location. It can also incorporate social media activity, such as tweets and check-ins on Foursquare or Facebook Places. This makes them very engaging for cross-platform promotions.

Full integration between location and social communities can increase the effectiveness of location-based advertising by social media, viral effects, and recommendations from friends by word of mouth. All these are powered by the context of real-time location updates. Social communities are more accessible and are always sharing information.

*   *   *

In the various ways outlined above, marketers can develop their knowledge of the use of mobile marketing and integrate it with social media technologies. By combining both, and with an understanding of how we can apply these tools and technologies to your business, you will be able to set the path for successful, integrated, and profitable business processes and digital campaigns.

Business Branding Through Mobile Social Media Communication Channels

Mobile social media sites offer excellent venues to promote a product or service for a business. By using these sites properly, a bond is developed between the business and the user. Businesses may set up both mobile and social media site profiles and pages, on which they can market their services or products. They can also be used to answer questions and make the site more interactive.

Advertisements on social networking sites are producing better results at a lower cost compared to other forms of advertisement. One effective strategy is to put advertisements on Facebook, which is able to help focus on targeted groups. Among the mobile apps, social location marketing tracked advertisements is another popular method for effective advertisement. This is a proven and effective method for product promotion, for both social media and mobile marketing.

HyperLinks (that are related to the promotion or advertisements) can also be posted on the social media sites. This makes it easier for someone to check out a business's website. As users click on the links, back links are created which can help to improve a business's page ranking.

As users visit the website and share it with their other friends, the traffic to the site will steadily increase. Increased traffic means a potential increase in revenue. All of this traffic will increase automatically; as the site is shared, it will give the business free advertisement and product promotion.

It is of the utmost importance that you develop a brand for your business. This involves the practice of creating recognizable sites with a good and prominent logo and a color scheme that can be easily identified. There should always be a personal or corporate brand with your product or business.

Users will begin to recognize you or your business as they are exposed to the same photo, logo, or avatar over and over again. They will be more likely to do business with someone they recognize. Normally, a person has to view a brand or logo at least five to eight times before they become aware of the brand.

Branding includes the effort of publicity, awareness, recognition, and the power of word-of-mouth recommendation.

Mobile and Social Networks provide an outlet where businesses can create and share contents and setup conversations. This means getting your brand name in front of your potential customers in order for them to recognize your brand and learn about it.

So, how can we position ourselves to take part in this digital branding age? Firstly, think of it as just another form of marketing. It can be easily integrated into most social media platforms. At the very least, you should be on Social network services like Facebook, LinkedIn, Twitter, Weibo, Renrenor Foursquare and Zappo for Mobile marketing.

Those running business should learn how to apply the tools of social media and study the behavioral profiles of target customers. Try to learn about their needs and find out about potential competitors.

If you decide to focus on branding, you will need a clear strategy. You will need ideas and methods to keep your sites and products in front of the public eye.

Tracking your statistics is vital. Many businesses that I communicate with have no idea how many people visit their website and where they come from. Social media, if used correctly, will increase your site traffic by an average of 10%.

Follow the checklist given to develop smart social brandings. Be consistent throughout all of your sites, handouts, or profiles. Aim to achievebrand awareness, brand recognition, and brand loyalty . . . .

Popular Content Creation and Sharing Sites in the World

Consider and analyze the available social networking services that can enhance your social media and mobile marketing program.

In some countries, access to a personal computer is less common, and this has been replaced with surfing the internet using the mobile phone.

Consider the following mobile social media tools and social network services to support your branding program:

- **Content Creation (Post)**

    Wordpress, Blogger, Multiply, Movable type, Livejournal, Hubpages, Youtube, Typepad, Vimeo, Tubemogul, Flickr, Squidoo, articlebase, articlesnatch, Docstocs, Scribd, Goarticles, and slideshare

> ### Asia-pacific popular sites:
> SOSO, Baidu, wenke, Sinablog, Yahoo Blog, MSN, Weibo, Kaixin, Docin (China); Orkut (India); Yam.com, Pixnet (Taiwan); Yahoo.hk (Hongkong); Friendster (Malaysia/ Philippines/International); and Stomp (Singapore)

- ## Content Sharing (Social Bookmarking)

There are hundreds of social bookmarking services with thousands of Pligg sites.

Depending on your time and available budget, content sharing tools are one of the more effective methods of sharing your content online. Some of the sites with PR rankings of 6 to 8 are:

Twitter, Digg, Reddit, Delicious, Propeller, Newsvine, Faves, Diigo, Tumblr, Plurk, Stumbleupon, Mixx, Jamesport, Jumptags, and Kirsty

> ### Asia-Pacific popular sites:
> Douban, Kaixin, Baidu, Weibo (China); Mixi (Japan); Friendster (Malaysia/Philippines/Internationally); Pixnet (Taiwan)

- ## Community with Connection Through SNSs (Social Networking Sites)

  Ning, Eacdemy, Facebook, LinkedIn, Google Plus, Google Buzz, Bebo, Xanga, Orkut, Xing, Viadeo, Netlog, Badoo, Twitter, V Kontakte (Russia), and Fotolog

  Asia-Pacific SNS:
  REN REN, KIAxin, QQ, Weibo, Baidu (China); Pixnet, Wretch.cc (Taiwan); Friendster and Orkut (India)

- ## Mobile Social Media on the Go

  Foursquare, Gowalla, Yelp, Loopt, Google latitude, Brightkite, Mocospace, Rummble, Zintin, Facebook, Frengo, Twango, MoBlog (UK), Orange World, Imity (Denmark) and Faceparty (UK)

  Asia-pacific mobile social media:
  Cyworld (Korea), Tencent QQ (China), EzMoBO (Taiwan), Mixi (Japan), MOBS (India), and Fropper (India)

CHAPTER 6

Develop a Mobile Social Media Marketing Plan for your Business

Internet users now spend more than 38% of their time online on social networks among the major economies like the US, China, and Europe. Therefore, it is important that businesses should explore how they can engage with their customers. Companies can get involved in conversations among their target markets, and the branding efforts can help companies gather supporters, build customer loyalty, and spread brand awareness.

As marketers, branding efforts include setting up the goal for your social media strategy;this should be based on your company's objectives, goals, and aspirations.

It is recommended to start with a gentle approach, as it will be easier to mitigate risks by starting with a small media strategy to gain confidence before engaging with more complex social media programs.

To start off, it will be best to analyze your objectives again, study all the tools of social media, and develop a mobile social media marketing plan.

As most of the online tools are free, marketers will still need to have some knowledge of how to use them. When working on a social media strategy for a business or branding, the following are some common strategies that should be applied:

A) Secure Your Brand

The first step for a successful Mobile and social media plan is to secure your brand. This should be done regardless of whether or not you plan to use it. It is important that you have control of your identity throughout theinternet. Register a good user name with some relation to your branding requirements.

Consider the following steps to build a full-fledged social media marketing program running full swing with a time-line for progressive steps:

- Set and define goals, objectives, and strategies
- Plan for a team to be trained on social and mobile media understanding and its structure.
- Select and determine a marketing team to be in-charge, it could be either to internally selected, a social media consultant, or both.
- Set up accounts with important social networking services and mobile platforms. The requirements should be determined depending on your market and demographics with major sites like SinaWeibo and RenRen for China; Facebook; Foursquare; LinkedIn; Twitter; and YouTube (see later chapters for different categories).
- Build your communities of clients, prospects, and influencers on the main social media sites listed (in

following chapters), on niche social and mobile media sites, and on established industry blogger sites.

- Boost your blog awareness with good contents like videos, podcasts with social bookmarking, and article submission efforts; ready your blog to be more mobile-content-compatible with some QR codes program or implementation of apps.
- Pay close attention to each relevant online community.
- Establish and develop groups of followers, both online and mobile.
- Create contents, such as a blog (which is ongoing), videos, white papers, podcasts, and more.
- Track development and generate progress reports.

Because social media revolves around so many free tools, and because it has become the darling of marketers everywhere, expectations are running high. However, do take note that it is evolving every day. There will be a major learning curve, with the consideration of language barriers, technology, culture, and niche features, along with the rise and fall of the various social media sites that are available around the world.

To implement and accomplish a good social media marketing plan will require considerable resources.

Every business and marketers must be ready to be open to requests for help, whether for training, people's time, or budget to pay for consultants, website hosting fees, a video camera, or useful web applications.

Finally, Social Media is a vast universe of communities, involving different cultures. Ultimately, for the marketer, it very much depends on which markets they are targeting to implement the right plan. As the tools of social media technology are no longer lead by the English language platform, a wider range of languages are advisable to push international penetration.

B) Integrating Online Marketing Tools for your Mobile and Social Media Strategy

The following will introduce some of the more popular tools of social media marketing. However, many other tools available online can be used for social media and mobile marketing. The tools mentioned in this book will also evolve over time, as newer tools will always change the landscape. Some less popular tools can reach a broader audience, while others reach a more highly focused niche audience. You will need to test the tools that are not discussed in the book as well. As long as the tools are able to help reach their targeted audience, they will be of help to marketers and identify the right audiences to spark communities and connect more effectively.

The common tools will be organized into categories. Chinese social media tools will be emphasized as well:

1) **Blog Communities**
   Wordpress, Typepad, Movable type, Vox, Blogcataklog, MyBloglog, Bloglines, Blogged, B5Media

Popular Chinese sites:
Sina Blog, Sohu Blog

2) Search engines

Google, Yahoo, Bing, Altavista, AOL, YouTube, etc.

Popular Chinese sites:
ASKBaidu, Baigoogle

3) Mobile search engine

m.google, Yahoo, Bing, Ask, Livesearchmobile, ASK, Kannuu, Just Dial (India), etc.

Popular Chinese sites:
Easou, Guanxi

4) Social networking Services

Facebook, Myspace, Hi 5, Orkut, Google Plus, Friendster, Netlog, Mixi (Japan), Cyworld (Korea), Wretch.cc (Taiwan), Hyves.nl (Holland), Studivz (Germany), Badoo (UK), Piczo (UK), Migente (Latin America), Werkennt-wen

Popular Chinese sites:
Qzone, RenRen, Pengyou, Sinaweibo, Kaixin001, 51.com, Douban, Taomee, Jiayuan

5) Microcommunities
Twitter, Friendfeed, Plurk, Yammer, Jaiku

Popular Chinese sites:
Kaixin001, Fanfou, Tencent Weibo, Sohu Weibo

6) Message Board (Forum)
Grouply, Google groups, Yahoo Answer, Mahalo Answer, Ezboard, DMOZ, Pinterest

Popular Chinese sites:
Tianya, Xici, Maopu

7) Business Networking
LinkedIn, Plaxo, Ecademy, Ryze, Viadeo, Xing, Connects, Hooversconnect

Popular Chinese sites:
Ushi, Tianji, Wealink

8) Review and Ratings
Yelp, Epinions, Brightscope

Popular Chinese sites:
Dianping, The Beijinger

9) **Location-Based/Mobile marketing**

Loopt, Foursquare, Rummble, Buddycloud, Jaiku, Komoo, Zannel, Gowalla, Brightkite, Friendticker (Germany), Nowhere.de (Germany), Goggle Latitude, Twitter Places, Yahoo-Koprol (Asian), Nejari (Korea), Tackable (Photo-based), Thegrid (Africa), Toai (Brazil)

Popular Chinese sites:
Zheli, Jiepang, Play4f, Kaikai

10) **Video and Live casting**

YouTube, Metacafe, Vimeo, Blip.tv, Blastro, Castpost, Dailymotion, Google video REVVER, vSocial, clip.vn (Vietnam), Veoh, Vision.Ameba.jp (Japan), Video.vol.at, Lustich (Germany), Luegmol.ch (Swiss), Wideo.fr (French), Miloop.se (Sweden)

Popular Chinese sites:
Video.qq, Youvideo.sina.cn, Youku, Tudou, 6.cn, Uume, Aeeboo, Youmaker

11) **Documents and e-content**

Scribd, Slideshare, Issuu.com, Docstoc, Hubpages, Squidoo, Calameo, Grin.com (Germany), Wobook, doxtop (Germany)

Popular Chinese sites:
Wenku Baidu, Docin, 360.cn, i.ask.sina, ccebook.cn, bookfm, shucang.niudown

12) Wikis

Wikia, PBWiki, Wiki, Social Text, Qwika, WikiMatrix (Germany), Scholarpidea, Wikipedia, About.com, Mahalo

> **Popular Chinese sites:**
> BaiduBaike, Hudong, Zhidao-baidu, sosobaike, Hexunbaike

13) Pictures and photograph

Flickr, Photobucket, Smugmug, Snapfish, Tinypic, Picasa

> **Popular Chinese sites:**
> Yupoo, Poco, Bababian, Badidou

15) Social Bookmarking

Diggo, Delicious, Stumbleupon, Evrnote, Reddit, Jumptag, Faves, Folkd, Digg, Mixx, Yahoo-buzz

> **Popular Chinese sites:**
> QQShuqian, BaiduShoucang, Jiathis, Diglog, bShare, Passit, Mister Wong, Qzone

16) Audio and Pod Casting

iTunes, Podcastalley, Talkshow, Odeo, Digital Podcast, Podast.de (Germany)

> **Popular Chinese sites:**
> ChinesePod, Podbean

17) Instant Messaging (IM Mobile-Enabled)

Skype, MSN, Googletalk, Whatsapp, Yahoo@Messenger

Popular Chinese sites:
Mobile Wangwang, QQ Mitalk, Weixin, Fetion

18) Connecting with Friends/Dating

Classmates, ConnectU, Friends Reunited, Graduates, Meetup, MyYearbook, Reunion, SKOUT, Googlefriendconnect, Match, Cupid

Popular Chinese sites:
Jiayuan, Zhenai

19) Question and Answer

Yahoo! Answers, Answers.com, Answer bag, All experts, Mahaloanswer

PopularChinese sites:
BaiduZhidao, Wenwen.soso

20) Mobile Social Network

Dodgeball, Freindstribe, Groover, Loopt, Gypsii, Mozes, Peepsnation, Wattpads, Mobikade, Mobagetown (Japan), Next2freinds.com

Popular Chinese sites:
China Mobile, Weibo, Sina, QQzone

Building communities using the tools mentioned above is an effective way to facilitate conversations and listen to feedbacks. With social media, marketers will need to participate in order to build relationships and connect to customers, prospects, influencers, and friends. Branding itself cannot build bridges; social media converse with people who are the representatives or users of the products.

Increase Visibility with Social-Bookmarking

When developing an effective content strategy, one is no longer restricted to web content. With the explosion of mobile social media as a whole, it has become increasingly critical to consider how your marketing strategy works in these new channels.

More and more, people are browsing for content not only on their computer but also on mobile devices. Now, with digital tablets like the Amazon Kindlefire and the Apple's iPad, the digital paradigm has expanded into more options. *How do you plan your content for your SNSs like Weibo or Facebook, where the conversation changes and evolves every day? How do you determine the right content for your YouTube account, or on your website? How do you make it suitable for your Mobile content sharing?*

Which will be the right channel to distribute your content, and how can we measure its success rate? In the following chapter, we will explore the different social media channels and how to integrate them into your content strategy. It is important to discover the importance of social bookmarking and content sharing and develop an effective integrated content strategy across today's digital media.

Content Sharing as a Strategy

There are various critical steps for optimizing your website's position for search engine rankings. These include using blogs, social networking systems (SNS), QR Codes, content sharing, and social bookmarking sites.

The previous chapters in this book have looked at the main blogs and SNSs and group strategies to promote your business.

Content sharing sites are sites that share a wide-variety of information, which includes video, QR codes, audio, text documents, PDFs . . . in fact, anything with digital content for both mobile and social media platforms.

There are many content sharing sites that allow content to be surfed on the web through your PC as well as your mobile devices. They include YouTube, Flickr, Phonefav, m.slideshare, Scribd.com, and Squidoo.

Content sharing can be in the form of written articles to share with others who are looking to learn from the Internet. Many expert authors and publishers use article sites like article base, Ezine, Articlesnatch, and GoArticles. They help to disseminate and share their content with other people who have similar interests.

Content sharing sites like m. slideshare have recently launched their mobile "on-the-go" version. These have attracted a huge number of visitors and subscribers. Viewers hit on these pages every month for the latest presentations or reports on specific industries or products.

Other major sites are Bukisa, Scribd, Hubpages, Squidoo, Baidu, wenke, Docin, and iask.sina. They have document uploading features, while others include video, audio, PDFs, spreadsheet, JPG, GIF, Word documents, and pictures in their various formats.

Often, these sites can embed your documents into your blogs, Facebook, Twitter, and other social media with mobile integration features.

To be totally effective in such diverse formats, these sites usually have large capacity storage areas to allow you to upload as much as you want.

Many sites also allow you to determine the access you wish to give to your guests. This way, you can share your content with everyone and be in public access groups.

Mobile Social Media: Engage Anytime, Anyplace

Finally, content sharing sites are extremely useful in creating healthy backlinks for improving search engine rankings. Many of these sites also allow you to link directly into the other social media in your portfolio of strategies, which may include external social media sites like Facebook, Twitter, and Sina Weibo.

Different types of Content sharing methods through mobile social strategies

With the latest iPhone and Smartphone technology, there are many possibilities for creating and sharing digital multimedia content when using your mobile phone and sharing information with friends and business acquaintances. This content can be shared phone-to-phone or via the QR codes and direct access to the internet.

Using a smartphone, users can:

- Capture images and upload to their social networking account;
- Create slide presentations and video footage, and share online;
- Share photo and pictures between friends through smartphones;
- Practice microblogging or tweet to similar groups of friends.

As most smartphone users can easily access the internet, they function well in:

- Making quick updates to your campaign or blog/website;
- Sending updates to micro-blogging sites, such as Twitter, Weibo, and Plurk;
- Uploading content to content-sharing services (such as YouTube and Flickr) using mobile software such asShozu, or through their social networking services.

In most developed countries, mobile phones are considered the alternate "third screen" in mobile social media as they are being increasingly used to access the internet while on the move. In certain countries with wireless-compatible phones, it is also possible to access the internet on your phone through free wireless "hotspots." Hotspots can be found at cafés, shopping malls, and that allows real-time events to be shared on line wherever and whenever there is access to the Internet.

Content Sharing on Social Media with QR Codes

QR Codes which has a background in tagging and hasbeen used in 2D barcoding used in production and management of data inventories since the early 2000s, has been slightly modified with "Social Sharing" in mind for use in mobile-related technology. A QR code can be read with a smartphone scanner or a 2D datamatrix barcode reader, and represent exciting possibilities for mobile data sharing.

QR codes can be easily generated with some Code generation sites likeKaywa, Delivr, BeetagBeQrious, Azonmedia, maestro, mobilefish, Quickmark, chinamobile (China), and goQR.me.

In the Mobile social media world, QR codes help customers to keep in touch through both the social web and mobile media.

Marketers can generate QR codes that make it easier for the target audience to share offline content such as special event information, trade show booth locations, books, or magazine articles with their social networks. Such offline content usually comes in the form of a tag sticker, which it can be placed at a prominent location. This can be near to the reception desk or at a tag verification counter, where the enquirer can always snap and scan the tag code to search more details online of the profile linked to the tag using their mobile phone. Data can include contact address, product information or specification, or even pricing.

A QR Code

QR Codes: Sharing Content with Communities online

QR codes have proven to be effective in building social communities offline as many people who own a smartphone are always ready to try out the QR codes scanning to familiarize themselves with the technology. One common application is to create a QR code that allows your audience to "like" or recommend your Facebook page from their mobile devices.

QR codes are also commonly used for product, branding, software applications, or location-based campaigns.

One useful application for marketers is to create QR codes that link to user-generated reviews of products or blog posts. This can help marketers build credibility with prospects and allows other to judge and review their content.

Good Positioning and Placement of QR codes

Scanning a QR barcode of software products like mobile apps on a computer screen to be shared with friends on a social network is common among smartphone users.

However, there are others who are used to desktop surfing and may still stick to using toolbars and share buttons. Therefore, net user may become subjective; thus, in order to use a QR code effectively, it must be placed at a positionthat will be noticed by your target audience.

There is quite a wide range of applications for effective usage of QR codes. Some examples include placing the code tags on physical venue locations. There are also QR code tags that are mounted on side doors or booth locations, and codes that are printed on brochures or stickers where target customers may chance upon them.

The following is a list of common locations for QR code placement:

- Urban advertisements located on billboards, signage on highways, shopping malls, etc.
- Business cards, brochures, catalogues, and direct mail pieces
- Convention and event signage
- Product tags and packaging
- Commuter buses, mass transit, trucks, and trailer signage
- Event tickets, coupons, venue ticket, etc.

QR codes are quickly becoming one of the fastest, easiest, and lowest-cost ways to link your offline advertising with your online community and content.

Proper and effective usage of QR codes in your offline marketing will allow marketers to boost awareness of their offline media to build on their online reach to potential customers. Thus, it will help to grow your e-mail list, deepening your engagement with your community, and boost customer and prospect satisfaction with your brand and products.

CHAPTER 7

Social Bookmarking Goes Social with online content sharing

Online content that is published by you is one of the most valuable information to share with your communities on the web. By sharing your content online, you can enhance your company's brand, broadcast your message across the web and demonstrate your expertise.

The most common way for websites to share content in the past is throughsending an email to their contacts with a link to the contentwhich you can click on and the content is shared.

By encouraging your readers to share your content with others is a really an effective way to drive targeted traffic to extend your brand and to drive traffic to your website or blog.

With the adoption of social media progressing at high speed, having simple content sharing tools such as social bookmarking buttons on your blog or website have proven to be effective tools for engaging social media.

Social bookmarking is more or less a by-product of blogging but it is based on the same basic technology. It is a way to share your favorite sites with others, advertise your own sites, and bring in traffic bolstering Search Engine Optimization (SEO).

Social bookmarking sites such as Delicious, Blinklist, diigo, dilog (China), allow their users to upload their own favorite site bookmarks so everybody else in the world can see and use those bookmarks. When a user uploads his favorite site bookmarks into his online account, a backlink is created to the site. As the number of people who click on the link increases, the site that has been bookmarked gets indexed and gains in ranking by the search engines.

This form of user driven advertisement is far more successful than any kind of paid advertising. There are many social bookmarking and Pligg sites on the Internet. New software is being developed all the time making these sites more and more productive as advertising and traffic driving tools.

So how do I increase traffic?

There are many ways in which you could increase your traffic: Such as using blog commenting tools, social bookmarking, article submission, rapid indexing, scrapebox harvesting and etc. We will elaborate further on two general methods which are considered as healthy practices and acceptable by Google.

1) **Free Backlink Method**
   In the first method, marketers will have to work extra hard. Most of your backlinks will be done and created by you.

You will have to create and post articles to multiple blogs and article submission websites. The method of article submission usuallyhas a snowball effect. Once the articles are posted, it will be there for as long as the website is available to the public. The rest will depend on netizens and users who are searching and finding articles which are related to their needs. This is generally a process which will take longer, and the targeted audience will be general public readers.

Article submission when done right, will help you to create backlinks on the article submission site to you blog or website, and when multiple readers click on your articles to read each time, it will have an auto-pilot effect and it helps to increase traffic consistently over time.

Sites to put on articles/videos for free:

- Wordpress
- Youtube,
- The Free Ad Forum
- Articles Yard,
- Articlesnatch
- Scribd
- Slideshare
- Baidu
- Wenku
- Docinetc

For Chinese Media sites, there are many websites that allow anonymous article submission and video submissions. Most of the Chinese sites will require proper registration either with an email or a QQ code before submission as China do have strict rules for uploading content to the social web.

2) **Paid advertisement**

This is a more direct approach. Here you would just have to fork out cash to purchase ads like advertising banners, engaging search engine optimization specialist, Facebook ads and Google Adwords. The responses for these methods are usually effective; you will get a sudden boost in your traffic and it would be mostly targeted to the group of audience which you are interested in. With all these traffic, your newly created products can be put to the test immediately as well.

Although this method is effective, it is usually expensive and only justifiable if the marketers have sufficient budget to run each campaign.

With the traffic flowing in continuously, it may seem good. But how many of your visitors are really buying your products and services? How many are just plain visitor who comes and goes. You need to set up a monitoring system in order for you to know whether you are making money from these tools. Otherwise, it would be just extra costs being incurred on your end and your business profit is not going to go up at all.

Tools to Help Get Paid Traffic:

- Google Adwords, Adbrite, clicksor, Bitvertiseretc
- Search Engine Optimization

- Advertising Banners on other relevant websites
- Radio/TV Advertising
- Admob, mojiva, admobile Mobile advertisement

Who is Using Social Bookmarking?

Social bookmarking becomes social when your shared content is visible to other users who use the same social bookmarking tools that you use.

Businesses have found it a good way to introduce themselves. Once a business website is listed on someone's favorite list, each viewer can see the website, visit it and get to know the business. Since it was 'referred' by a friend, they are more likely to use the site or buy something from it.

Networks of friends can be set up so that whenever a new posting is made to a social networking site of other members of the network are notified immediately by RSS feed. This allows for rapid circulation of a story, advertising or a website.

You can see why it is important for those who are involved in Internet marketing to be in touch with social bookmarking sites with all of these instant communications made between users.

Innovative marketers join sites such as Friendster, Facebook, Linkedin, RenRen or MySpace. In doing so, they can have fun socializing and at the same time, they are also selling their products and services. By becoming a part of the social circle, they have become more trustworthy or a friend.

More importantly, they get visitors to their websites. Because of this influx, they are improving their Page Rank with the search engines. Business owners have found social bookmarking to be one of the best search engine optimization tools that have come along in a very long time.

Does Social Bookmarking Work for Mobiles Too?

The basic concept of mobile social marketing is that it is user-directed. Social bookmarking is a way of organizing and categorizing information by using 'tags' on Desktop, while the mobile platform is a newer concept that is gaining popularity. It tends to Use "Places"—Post Places, Share Places—Get Places.

Tags are user generated and are based upon keywords which identify the bookmarks and offer categorizing and labeling system that enables Internet users to categorize the contents. These include web pages, online photographs, and web links as well.

This is a true user-directed way to organize and categorize information. When you try to retrieve your favorite from a List of bookmarks, the tag function will help you to sort the sites under a chosen tag which you nominated. You do not need to remember where you placed your links.

There are many web tools, and thousands of Social bookmarking sites which allow the easy creation of Social Bookmarks. Simply register with a sites like:

- www.delicious.com
- www.shuqianqq.com

- www.diglog.com
- www.digg.com
- www.reddit.com

You can store social bookmarks and add tagging (the categorizing exercise) to make finding these sites easier for everyone. Visitors to these websites can quickly find your social bookmarks by searching for websites by such criteria as keywords, phrases, tag-related to your subject interest.

Contents of social websites like, Propeller, delicious.com and digg.com will allow people to share their favorite websites with others. In most cases, they would enable for additional comments. It is becoming increasingly common for websites to include icons or links to the most popular social tagging sites to encourage visitors to tag them, with the aim of generating more site traffic.

Mobile social bookmarking has various version of bookmarking method. The common type is similar using mobile friendly sites like Digg with their mobile apps where their mobile site is optimized to run on pretty much any mobile browser. Logging in to browse and Digg your favorite stories and view a sample of the top comments for each story, will be similar to Tagging to Bookmark.

Well, with new advancements in the social and mobile integration, mobile-info-center sets off and develop the PhoneFavs which is a new mobile web portal. It provides social bookmarking system to deliver mobile-friendly content across to friends on the mobile devices.

PhoneFavs is available and free. It works similarly alongother social bookmarking tools of which its function is to store and share your bookmarks. No matter if you are on a desktop or texting away at the airport, you can also add tags, titles and other social bookmarking markers if needed.

Another major social bookmarking service provider who has recently launched this application is "Addthis" fromClearspring who focus their application for the iPhone, iPad, iPod Touch and various Android devices. Their AddThis Application will let native iOS application developers better integrate social sharing functionality on their apps for their mobile platform.

Mobile social bookmarking has various bookmarking methodsanother recently popular method has come to light and it makes uses mobile location-based bookmarking technology with mobile apps technology, popular sites are like Flager and Favspot which allows you to send a text or picture message with your location and plot it on a Google Map and user can bookmark the places where they have gone before.

Users will be able to check on bookmarked locations through recent check-ins from other users, the friends you're following, and also nearby locations. The saved locations can either be a place you checked-in to or bookmarked or favorited by another user. Favspot, however, allows you to simply save a friends location rather than doing a check-in.

Other similar Mobile Bookmarking sites include;

- Mobiseer.mobj (mobile)
- PlacesTodo (mobile)
- Flagr.com (mobile)

How is Social Bookmarking being handled with language barriers between the Western world and China

Due to unique implications and different language orientation, it is impossible to take social media from the West and simply integrate into Middle Eastern, European and especially China contexts.

While Europeans have an in depth history and culture with English language usage, they will not have much problem with language barriers. Whereas in the China market, tough adjustments by marketers from the West are needed to get into the Chinese internet world. This means they will need to embrace a deeper level of understanding for the Chinese identity and their lifestyle. Just to simply explain the basic difference, we will quote tagging as an example. The following are some tags described in the Chinese Language. They can be found in most article submission sites, blogs, microblogs and social bookmarking sites.

Tags in Chinese:

- Label (标签)
- Category (分类)
- eBook (电子书)
- Keyword (关键词)

Usually, they are shown in Chinese characters, without English translation and users will need to recognize them in order to differentiate them from other Chinese characters. The Chinese language can be complex especially for non-Chinese. Western marketers who can read Chinese and have a basic foundation of the Chinese language is in a better position to participate in China's internet landscape.

According to the latest data from Google's Adplanner website, we noticed that web portals likeRenRen, SinaWeibo, Sohu or QQ rank among the top favorite sites in China. These local Internet Chinese portals offer a wide array of social media services, from SNS, forums, instant messaging, blogging, photo and video sharing, to free email addresses and comprehensive social networks.

As the majority of China Netizens are young users, the trend to using mobile social media has caught up between the Western and Chinese world. Hence, this has encouraged many developers to create special software applications and social networking services which have millions of members like the following social networking service platforms:

- RENREN
- SinaWeibo
- Tencent
- Kaixinwang001

As microblogging and social networking servicesexpand in China, with their SNS space fills up with well over 200 million consumers engaging with thousands of brands, RenRen, Weibo with other multiple large and established players are now China's leading dynamic internet landscape.

As these players are investing for long term growth providing full fledge services, they are at the forefront of marketers' minds and a fundamental requirement in branding strategies. In order to ensure effective use of Weibo and RenRen to market brands and engage with their targeted audience will require proper understanding of the platform, local culture, user profiles and their behaviors.

China has the largest Internet population in the world with almost 390 million users. (forecasted to hit 488 Million by 2015) It has a huge audience who isvery actively involved especially in the usage of internet technology such as, viewing of video, playing online-games and engaging online for sharing.

Its digital media technology has evolved with much developments occurring independently from the rest of the world. This is caused by major language barriers within the Chinese mobile social media landscape. With its size and its culture, new trends will start to develop as it progresses further. Sometimes, making it difficult for Western developers to fully adopt their technology and pushing it across other platforms and social networking sites.

China is already trying to cater to the niche—the mobile social media behaviour and activities. Therefore, in order for the western Social media to be able to captivate the Chinese Netizens, they will need to find local partners to cooperate to develop their SNS and microblogging sites to suit and attract the Chinese community and yet function similar for their western net user.

One majorly successful SNS platform is Mister Wong. It is a social bookmarking service, which has a strong following in China and is actually owned and ran by a German corporation.

Here are some of the effective social bookmarking sites in China, which can be found at the Addthis platform at http://www.addthis.com which includes:

- Kaixin
- Douban
- Qzone

For a detailed and compiled list of the top social bookmarking sites that can be accessed at Addthis's service directory. Emarketers can find up to 330 high ranking social bookmarking sites for their use.

"Addthis" social bookmarking service makes it easy for website visitors to share their websites and mobile contents on many social networks. With AddThis, your audience can promote your content by sharing up to 330 of the most popular social networking and bookmarking sites (like Facebook, Twitter, Digg, StumbleUpon and MySpace). It provides a plugin widget and also support address bar sharing for the most modern browsers. This way it will be easier to add to your website or blog, and it offers weekly analytics on pages or posts shared

Widget tools in sharing; RSS Feeds, Wiki, Share and Like Buttons

In the world of mobile social media, widgets appear in a wide range of places. Many bloggers and users of social networking sites will make use of widgets to make their sites more interesting and fun for their users. A widget may do any number of things, from organizing a blogpost by topic to allowing people to play interactive games with other users of a website. These widgets are usually developed by third parties, and **can be embbed or copied onto the owner's website, and then inserted on a blog (Blogger, Wordpress, Twitter, etc . . .) and on social networks (facebook, Folkd, Netvibes, Faves, etc . . .) at your convenience.**

Widgets are useful content sharing tools which can **help to increase traffic exponentially on the internet.** The following will provide a brief introduction of some of the common widgets used in social networking:

- **Share Buttons:**
  Add this uses their share button widget and has been installed on almost 1.2 Million sites throughout the World, and this has prompted other platforms to provide similar services which include:

  Sharethis, Social Marker, Addto any, Onlywire, Seitzeichen. de (Germany)

Baidu Share, Jiathis, bShare (China)

"Share button" feature allows a viewer to click on a share button and share an article or website with a particular friend or with a circle of friends.

This feature allows a group of like-minded individuals to view material or information of interest without each one having to perform a separate search.

One of the main benefits of having a share button on your website is to increase traffic. Each time a person 'shares' your website with their friends, more traffic will be brought to your website increasing your potential sales and your possible page ranking.

The group is also a focused target group since the visitor sharing your website with the group has similar or like interests. Focused visitors are even more likely to increase your sales revenue.

- **Like Button:**

Facebook and RenRen software designers have developed a widget to allow you to place a "Like" button on each separate article you write on your blog or website, on videos you may have included, or even on the advertisements you may have.

Each time a user views one of the items and clicks on the like button; the system automatically makes a post on their

Facebook page and notifies all of their Facebook friends they found something they like.

This is free advertisement for the website owner which may generate more traffic and increase their page rankings. If each visitor has just 10 friends that receive the notification and each of those friends visits your site and 'likes' it .... I'm sure you can see how it could build very quickly.

- **RSS Feed:**
  The acronym RSS stands for Really Simple Syndication and is yet another Web 2.0 feature allowing the web to be user-driven rather than by the powers-that-be. Users subscribe to these feeds to use RSS content and use reader or aggregator technology.

  The reader or aggregator checks the user's website so when the site has new content, it picks it up and sends it to the user. A client based reader or aggregator is a stand-alone program attached to an existing program such as a web browser or an email reader. A web-based reader or aggregator makes the user's feeds available on any computer with web access.

- **Wiki:**
  A short definition for Wiki is "Wiki is a piece of server software that allows users to freely create and edit Web page content using any Web browser. Wiki supports hyperlinks and has simple text syntax for creating new pages and cross-links between internal pages on the fly."

In short, Wiki technology allows editing of material posted on a website by the poster or by others.

The best example of Wiki technology action on the Internet is Wikipedia. In the old Web 1.0 way of doing things, the owner of a website had full control over all material that was posted to the website and only website owners could edit material posted on the website.

CHAPTER 8

The Smartphone—The Mobile Internet Device

Smartphones and mobile social media are affecting our lives immensely, especially in terms of communication and convenience of access to information.

Yes! I am just one of 800 million people globally who is having problems going anywhere without my mobile phone. With it, I can do tasks like checking emails and surfing the internet while catching up with my friends on social networking services.

Recent research from a major mobile analyst firm in the US in May 2012 has found that 80 per cent of smartphone users have access to email and around 73 per cent have accessed social networks via their devices based on mobile browser and app audience combined usage

What is interesting is that email usage is increasing, due to the social network usage on Mobile internet devices. Email has been the basis of content sharing since the early eighties. The reason for the recent increase is that users of smartphones can access them through mobile social media and keep in touch with their social network. By logging into the social networking sites or using email or messaging with special apps like "WhatsApp messenger," messaging applications or SMS are ways to encourage users to communicate and share at very low cost.

Marketer also need to appreciate all the new portable gadgets known collectively as "mobile-enabled internet devices." For example, iPad, Android-type Smartphones, or the Samsung Galaxy tab, and the most recent Amazon Kindle, are mobile communication tools. They can be used to open up communication channels with customers in the social web.

These devices will be able to help us build stronger relationships with customers, attract new customers, and to retain existing ones. Most units provide surfing features for both mobile marketing and social networking communication.

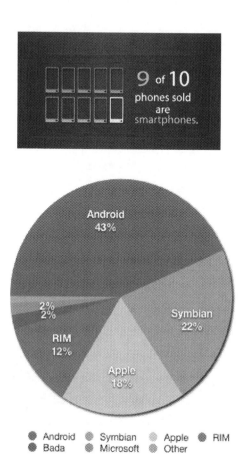

Graph showing Global Smartphone share at
the end of 2011

Furthermore these technologies can complement one another. The value of mobile social media and all the other communication apps like Whatspps, Viper, emailing, QR codes, andSMS combined can amount to a more successful campaign than when they are all executed individually. Here are a few key steps to take in order to optimize the success of integrated digital campaigns that include both mobile devices and social mobile elements:

1. **Make content mobile-accessible**

    First of all, the marketer should ensure that any digital content produced is compatible with and easily accessible by all mainstream mobile devices. Many business decisions are made away from the office. As a result, entrepreneurs or professionals using smartphone devices can access your content while travelling in train, subway, or on the highways

2. **Optimize your Blogspot Wordpress blog**

    It is also advisable to add in the functionality to share content through Facebooks groups, Twitter and your other social networking accounts wherever possible. If customers receive a mobile advertisement or an SMS of interest via their smartphone devices, they are encouraged to share your content with their own social network of friends. This helps to increase word-of-mouth marketing, which can also include a forum, bulletin board, or group where they can comment instantly on a particular topic or seek peer reviews and support.

3. **Mobile app—a creative content marketing tool**

    There are many developers who specialize in developing smartphone applications for both iOS and Android operating system. Usually, an application can be in the form of productivity tools, games apps, or office tools. The scope is wide, and it is extremely useful to run offers and promotional or discount codes for products and services through such applications to your loyal customers.

4. **Encourage customer engagement interactively at events.**

   At convention, seminar, or exhibition events, look to offer SMS short codes, inviting prospects to text for more information on a product or service, or even a QR code. An example would be, to scan QR codes in exhibits with a tag or encourage the prospects to text to receive the latest video of a product demonstration. When the prospect texts or scan the code, it will then automatically prompt them to enter an email address. A link to the video will be sent to them. Thus, data will be added to your customer relationship management system (CRM). As always, this digital content should be optimized to be shared immediately amongst social networks.

In the various ways outlined above, marketers can develop appropriate content for the use of mobile enabled internet devices, social networks, and smartphones. By combining this with a greater understanding of how we can apply these tools and technologies to our businesses, we can develop more successful, integrated, and profitable business processes and digital campaigns.

Therefore, in order to embrace mobile technology to be connected with their communities, consider the following tools to work with your smartphone:

- Facebook App
- Twitter App
- Foursquare or Gowalla, or Yelp apps

- Mobile video sharing apps, like Vimeo, Qik
- Mobile Images and photo sharing apps, like Instagram, Dailybooth, or Flickr
- Mobile Browser like Operan Mini orSkyfire
- Mobile group texting apps like Brightkite or Groupme
- Mobile QR code readers
- Mobile payment apps, like Mobile PayPal, Square Up, and Go payment
- Mobile social bookmarking apps

With such smartphone apps available, marketers can tweet from location, send messages, blog, and social bookmark to mobile social networksfrom anywhere with wireless internet connection.

Smartphones Enable Mobile and Digital Media Marketing

It is projected that by 2013 the number of mobile web users will surpass the number of desktop web users. Marketers will have to consider those mobile users and their specific needs or interests in planning their mobile social media marketing.

All those mobile users are going to be potential customers visiting your website, mobile site (mobisite), and blogs. The following could be some of the factors that shift web traffic to mobile platforms. This traffic will simply replace some of your existing online web traffic; even so, it is crucial that the transition is smooth in order to avoid losing traffic.

1. Mobile Email

Increasingly, people check their email on mobile phones. Businesses need to be prepared for the possibility that any email sent may be read on the screen of Mobile devices. It should exhibit many similar characteristics to when used on the desktop. You may want to follow all the best usability and accessibility rules . . .

Be brief and Be specific.

Your subject line is the key to getting your message opened, so use it effectively. Keep it within 30 characters or less. In your email format, consider using plain text; however, as we often want to make it pretty, we opt for HTML. Remember that email on a mobile device competes with SMS for messaging efficiency and for the user's attention.

2. Mobile Web Search

Mobile users will usually search for information using their mobile phones. It is a widely used function ofsmartphones and is growing every day. Search is the core component of every mobile web user's experience; this is the same for desktop users. However, with users being on the move, the locality function exceeds that of the desktop user. Mobile searchers have a higher tendency to be doing searches on and seeking things that are nearby. Therefore, searches should be linked to location-based functions.

Increasingly, people search, network, browse, and shop from a range of mobile devices. Consumers are choosing where to go and what to do based upon online recommendations and reviews from their friends, members, or groups from social networking sites—the people they trust the most. Presently, most search functions on mobile-devices are powered by Google Places or Yahoo Maps. Marketers now realize that a local search marketing strategy can also be converted into mobile marketing strategies, which include utilizing mobile coupon campaigns, QR codes, and proximity marketing.

Mobile search and tracking tools
Here are some tools and technologies that can provide easy access

- Movitas
- Bazaarvoice
- Radian 6
- Google Places

Once you are sure that consumers can easily find your physical location, look for online conversations and reviews to see how your business is faring with the public. Easy access on mobile internet devices and smartphone play a major part for your business. Marketers need to be ready to serve mobile devices because people are already searching on their smartphones on a daily basis.

3. **Mobile Social Media**
   Participation with social networking sites on mobile devices is getting popular, with their SNS apps available for free download on most smartphones. When we talk about mobile social media, we are really talking about Foursquare, Yelp, Twitter, Instagram, Facebook, Weibo and many others, which are boosting their presence. To be successful

in MSMmarketing, a good marketing plan is required to optimize, distribute, and track content across all mobile social platforms.

4. **Text Messaging (SMS)**

Text messaging remains the most common form of mobile marketing. Messages are usually no longer than 160 characters (including spaces and punctuations) and are sent directly to a mobile user through the mobile phone carrier network. Both Twitter and Facebook have a SMS component built-in, and they are the easiest marketing tools for your MSM marketing. There are other applications specifically made for the purpose of SMS. You can check out "WhatsApp", a new application that may replace the SMS for most smartphone users. It is mostly provided for FREE, and the messages you send are through the internet, so you do not need to pay for the services of your network carrier.

5. **Multimedia Messaging (MMS)**

The major difference between MMS and SMS is that the MMS is mainly for sending pictures or videos. MMS, like SMS can be used to send text; however, it can also include Multimedia files. It is able to embed links to mobisites, offer compelling coupons, and provide services to share photos, audio, and even videos.

6. **Mobile Apps**

These applications can be for entertainment or can serve as a useful function. Businesses can build their own apps or advertise on third party apps. Application with the most usable functions and relevance will be the most appreciated and will be installed by the greatest number of users. Nowadays, new mobile phones come pre-installed with apps. These usually include games, news, weather, banking or financial, entertainment, messaging, audio and video players, navigation, product reviews, shopping, and even apps for price comparison.

7. **Mobile LBS and Review**

Mobile technology used with the Location Based Service (LBS) utilizes GPS to generate geolocation awareness and to allow customers to check-in to a venue. Many venues and stores have noticed the potential for boosting their business by using the LBS. They have put up QR codes to allow mobile phone cameras to scan. This is so that users can share their location with friends through sites like Foursquare and Facebook. SNS further boosts the function to become more popular when users can use the check-in as part of a game.

Third party developers have introduced mobile applications with capabilities meant for major shopping stores. These include bar code scanning for quick access to product reviews and information that customers would like to view or voice their opinion upon. This drive and acceleration for the acceptance of mobile marketing technology has helped many companies to prosper.

8. **Mobile Video**

The use of mobile video as an advertising platform is fast becoming popular, especially for those seeking updates of the latest movie trailers or music videos for the On-the-Go Youth groups. The mobile video audience is set for rapid expansion with further expected improvements in new the mobile internet devices. This is trend is complemented with mobile broadband being made available and the emergence of better quality videos. The videos are provided by most carrier networks with improved mobile-video technology.

Changes in the mobile social media world is moving at an incredibly fast and accelerating pace. Consumers can easily connect to websites whenever they want to. Knowing and understanding your targeted audience is essential. Knowing who they are, what their wants and needsare, and where they hang out are your first steps when creating an effective marketing initiative for mobile social media marketing.

How Geolocation /Mobile Networking has changed the World

Smartphone with location-based services

Social media has changed the world and supercharged social action, online marketing, and social entrepreneurship. Indeed, its true value is not determined by the technology used to create it. Instead, it is valued more by how we use it to increase our productivity in both business and our way of life. Today, a second wave of innovation, which incorporates both mobile technology and social Media, is helping define a Web 3.0 era. This is setting the stage for change over coming years.

Mobile technologies integrated with social networking are extending the full online internet network to anyone with a mobile device or smartphone. This is done while enabling social networking, social action, and m-commerce to converge to form a location-based Social network.

The combination of smartphones, mobile broadband, and social networking allows users to interact, share, meet up, and recommend places based on their physical location. This real-world connection (through mobile devices) with social media can mean more visitor traffic and profits for proactive business owners.

As a start, you should at least have an understating of the concept behind the location-based social networks (or as they call it, the "Lo-so" applications). Most mobile device users are motivated to use "lo-so" apps while on the go. This is done through their smart phones and tablets to update their whereabouts by "checking-in" whenever they go to certain places. The phone's internal GPS locates the user's whereabouts and determines what possible "location" they could be at. This provides the user with options to allow friends to know where they are, or where they frequently go.

Users can also opt to send automatic updates to their SNSto stay connected. This way, both mobile networking and social networking services are interlinked.

Businesses are getting in on the fun by announcing specials or promotions with coupons, tips, or events through these apps. This is so that when users check-in they will receive notifications of nearby services providing special deals or promotions.

This way they could forge firm relationships and establish goodwill with local potential clients or create a presence for their social web connection of friends, family, co-workers, etc.

To be familiar with mobile social LBS, it is necessary to become familiar with the dominant platforms: Foursquare, MyTown, Gowalla, Loopt, Brightkite, PlacePop, Google Latitude, and even Yelp. These are the most talked about in general, though their popularity for usage varies by geography. Sign up for all of these and download the apps to your phone if you can. This is so that you can become familiar with how someone would use each app. Most of the networks have iPhone, Android, and BlackBerry apps, and all of them allow you to check-in via desktop and mobile web browsers.

Foursquare screenshot

Location tagging service

Businesses with physical locations stand to increase their local audience and further their market outreach. This can be done through geolocation platforms, which link real-world locations to the mobile devices.

Geolocation tagging is the process of topography enhancement; it uses geographical identification signature or metadata to digital media such as photographs, maps, IP address, or GPS co-ordinates, which usually consist of latitude and longitude coordinates.

Foursquare, BrightKite, Gowalla and Loopt are major location services that allow users to tag and check-in at locations. They also allow one to share and update status among a network of friends. By tagging your physical location(s), you can ensure that your business is discoverable on geolocation maps provided on their services.

Among the most popular "So-Lo-Mo" services, Foursquare provides niche features that allow for update check-ins, and it has a gaming element in which users earn badges and can work their way to becoming the "mayor" of their favorite locations. This has attracted users to their services, and advertisers have been able to gain exposure by using their services.

How can Geolocation Help your Business?

If you have a local businesses which very much depends on local customers, geolocation can help improve your business.

It can help you to localize information for your customers. For example, you can focus your marketing and promote to local people. Geolocation allows companies to show products and services that are available in particular areas.

In order to begin with the geolocation tagging of your business, consider building that location-tagging presence in that area. Figure out how to draw people in from nearby towns or cities into the particular area. One example would be, if you own a local cafe, you can use it to have people to "check-in" to the place. This will help spread the word and offer them a promotional discount on their coffee. Also, think about banding together with other local businesses to do cross-promotions that might benefit your area.

Make sure your business is already discoverable on geolocation apps.

First, visit a few "So-Lo-Mo" sites to check if your particular address and business category are listed there. If it is not, add it in or contact the social location services site to find out how you can get your business address and location added.

Your storefront businesses based on your geo-location coordinates can be geographically optimized and marketed through search engine marketing. The whole application is able to work on a real-time basis and provides dynamic interaction for contents generated in these location-based app spaces.

An example:

For a business, you can get started by claiming your site venue in Foursquare through the following URL:

- https://foursquare.com/business/merchants/claiming

This process will identify and verify your location, and also includes details the manager and business contact details.

After registering your venue site, proceed to create a "Special Campaign" or FREE "Promotional Gimmick." This can be in the form of any kind of special discount that you wish to provide. Gimmick special promotions are a good way to attract and reward customers. The special offer should make the person want to check-in to your place. This offers exposure of your business to nearby customers.

Foursquare will usually breakdown the statistical analysis into the following data. This will help the marketer to monitor on the results.

- Total daily check-ins over time
- Your most recent visitors
- Your most frequent visitors
- Gender breakdown of your customers
- What time of day people check in
- Check-ins that are broadcasted to Twitter and Facebook

Businesses are suggested to post a link to their Foursquare page on their website and Facebook page and Twitter as well. Post signage in the establishment itself provides customers with an easier way to find them on the location-tagged sites. This offers easy reference for all your customers.

Build loyalty programs

Once small businesses get well versed in the apps, they can begin to reach out to customers more effectively. Businesses can start with customer loyalty programs around the Gaming and Social Networking aspects of location tagging apps to reward loyal customers who use their services. You can also combine a loyalty program that rewards your existing customers with location-based services that offer rewards. This will help generate positive feedbacks for your products, services, and/or brand. With integration of data available from your social networking sites (like Facebook and Twitter), the loyalty program can be customized based on the following social data points:

- Location of client
- Target of your loyalty program
- Preference of brand or product
- Proximity and frequency of a potential client who will accept the offer to the places that person visits frequently
- Travelling habits of potential clients or places they like to visit
- Gauging clients' purchase behavior

CHAPTER 9

The Power of Mobile Social Media for Business

How to Be Successful Online—Social media and Mobile Media Optimization: Getting Noticed

The Social media landscape has grown far andway beyond sites like Facebook and Twitter. All types of mobile apps and social sites are now available to enable communication through images, video, content, etc.

Remember . . . it is all about the right content. Content is what keeps a visitor on your blog orwebsite, and content is what makes them return to your website. It is a well-known fact that purchases are seldom made on initial website visits.

A customer will likely return to the website up to seven times before he actually drags out his credit card and buys something. You have to get them to come to your website for that first crucial visit, but you must also keep them making those return visits.

A good way to keep them coming back is by giving them something to catch their attention, such as audio and video posts or podcasts. While it is true that people do read blog posts, people are more geared toward audio and video than toward the written word. Everybody watches television . . . a lot. Accordingly, picture and video being broadcast really is worth more than a thousand words in today's technology-centered world.

With many companies now having mobile social media marketing in place, social media optimization (SMO) will be the next logical step to improve the effectiveness of social mobile media marketing. For reference, Wikipedia defines SMO as "The methodization of social media activity with the intent of attracting unique visitors to website content."

The following are general rules that will help in SMO:

1) **Create and share your content**

Determine the content that your audience prefers to share across different social media platforms for blogs, websites, and mobile site. For mobile audiences, include your most important concepts phrases and keywords within the first 20 words. Make content brief but effective for mobile content.

2) **Make sharing easy**

This includes the embedding of buttons and other widgets to encourage sharing, recommending, or bookmarking within your website, mobile site, and blog. Always enable your mobile content users to tag and bookmark your content with the most popular social mobile media sites and tools. Add mobile bookmarking and tagging links and widgets to every page of your mobile site. Ensure a forwarding option enabled for your content so that a friend can forward to others.

3) Momash "mashup"

This process encourages users to take and combine your site's content with theirs so that it becomes user generated content. The same can be applied on mobile sites, where your users can use your mobile content for their own mobile websites (mosite), mobile blogs (moblog), mobile applications (moapp) or in any combination of the above.

These methods are useful for reviewing your approach to integrating social mobile media marketing into mobile and social platforms. This will help the marketer to determine from the practice some valuable data and characteristics of their customers. These include:

- Helping to identify influencers and seeding content
- Understanding which sharing activities and types of promotions lead to business results, leads, sales, or brand preference
- The frequency cycle that generates more viral activities
- Determining how social and mobile media can support SEO activities and encourage backlinks
- Determining which type of audiences use which social media platforms to share what kind of content and offers
- Determining different effective methods to integrate the sharing of content through different social platforms, web, mobile, and email channels

The Relationship between Mobile and Social Media

Web 2.0 is user-driven, and users are the ones who determine the success or failure of an internet business. Before exploring how to capitalize on social media for your business, it is best listen to what people are talking about and what may interest them . . . this is the very basis of familiarizing yourself with the social media landscape. Web surfers no longer simply go to websites to read information. They go to websites to GET information, and they prefer for that information to be delivered in audio and/or video formats.

In reality, there are many people who will utilize social networking and mobile marketing (mobile social media) for business. People who initially use it only for personal reasons often run into something that could help them in their business. Therefore, if marketers do not take the time and apply mobile social media to their business, they may miss out on a great deal of valuable exposure.

Audience Interaction

How much effort does it take to interact with your audience before your mobile social media is developed? You may have used a company event or trade show, which required a tremendous amount of resources to get started. Audience interaction was limited to the event and was almost non-existent after it was over. By engaging the audience on an on-going basis, you can build confidence in the relationship between the audience and your company. This will allow them to look at you in a whole new light.

Proactive Branding

Mobile social media allows your online brand to grow, as well as your search engine rankings. Companies are embracing the mobile social media platform to raise recognition of their company and their products while allowing their customers the opportunity to interact on their websites, blogs, and mobisites. This interaction builds confidence in the company brand and can be shared across the network through mobile social media.

Customer Service and Feedback—Example

Let us imagine that you own a Hair Salon that has been open for a few months, and business has been good. It has been doing so well you have paid off a few business debts and you take a week off for vacation. You keep in touch and also check your e-mail while away.

You are alerted to a negative post on your blog by a Google Alert you set up for your business. It seems someone had a poor experience at your salon and posted a negative comment on your blog. You're able to respond quickly to the person instead of letting the negative review become viral and influence others. By speaking directly to the blogger, you can diffuse the negative experience by offering free services.

Not only will this allow the blogger to try your service again, but it will show others your willingness to listen and how prompt you are to rectify any negative situation. Another Google Alert a few weeks later informs you the blogger wrote a follow-up post about your great customer service.

Lead Generation—Example

We can go further using the example of a new Hair Salon. Using Twitter Search, you can search for people chatting about a bad haircut they received within a certain distance of your salon. Once you find these chats mentioning a bad haircut, you can start a conversation, mention your salon, and then offer them a discount if they wish to have the haircut redone at your Salon. About 50% of the people you offer this coupon to will probably come in, and if you dazzle them with good work, about 40% of those new customers will come back for another haircut.

If you set up Flickr and YouTube accounts and maintained them properly since your grand opening, you should post a coupon code in a photo or video for you viewers to see. If you generate new leads, then you will get extra people coming in for haircuts each month.

Mobile social media multiplies the entry points for your brand and your business. Instead of customers finding your business through Google Search or the Yellow Pages, you have expanded the opportunities for additional business because new customers can now find you through Twitter, Yelp, Foursquare, Facebook, LinkedIn, YouTube, Flickr, and many, many more.

You also have the potential through the Facebook's "Like" button to generate new leads through the viewers that click on the button. The possibilities are endless for mobile social media marketing campaigns. Get creative and go for it!

How to Jumpstart Mobile Social Media Strategy

The example I gave for the Hair Salon is a simple one, but the basis for it can be used regardless of the business you wish to start. Your business may be a physical location with a sticker tag on your storefront office door with a QR code that needs to be promoted. It might be an online business, or maybe it is simply one digital product. For example, you may run a clothing store, have your clients take a picture trying your clothes, and encourage them to post it to Facebook and then remember to tag your store in the photo. State your URLS: make it easy for others to find your store.

Consumers have started to embrace social media with mobile interactions, mostly because the major social networks seem to have been developing opportunities for mobile-social users. Typically, any smartphone users would be keen to interact with their friends using the latest mobile internet devices. Therefore, mobile social media is already part of the mobile strategy.

Here are some simple but effective ways that can help you drive more social-mobile interactions with your business while we wait for the mobile social media landscaping to move forward with new emerging social mobile technologies.

However, before a business can take advantage of the power of mobility, it needs to optimize its marketing efforts to reach out to customers on the move. It is crucial to integrate a mobile initiative into your mobile social media strategy.

Here are some tips on how you can do so:

- Set up a Facebook page, a Twitter profile, a YouTube account, and a Flickr account . . . and don't forget Foursquare
- Cross-promote mobile initiative on SNS by posting keywords and short codes to your wall
- Use mobility to increase visibility of your social media message
- Engage with potential customers on Twitter, Weibo, Foursquare, Jiepang (China), and Facebook by running localized and real-time searches for people talking about your targeted niche or product
- Encourage users to use their mobile to text to follow

When you add a friend on Foursquare or Jiepang (China), you can view all of his or her check-ins. You can do the same on Facebook. These "check-ins" can help determine a friend's interest or preferences in the local scene.

Social Network services like Facebook and Twitter have built-in tools to enable users to share contents from their smartphones that can help to entice a larger number of users to participate in your own mobile social community. Twitter also has a free app available for most popular smartphones.

Build up a mobile data list by featuring a mobile widget on a customized Facebook/SinaWeibo page (as well as on your website). You can also send out SMS messages of promotions as part of the program.

The best way to get the most out of mobile social media is to align your marketing strategies using the latest social networking services available, along with mobile technologies. Social networking services like Twitter, Jiepang, Facebook, and Foursquare are supported by mobile devices. They are able to provide dedicated services like geo-location options and SMS services, which are essential for any updates on your products and services.

1. Considerposting videos and pictures to your YouTube account. Engage with pictures, videos, and other media. Encourage your customers to upload photo and videos as their ways of recommending your product to their friends.
2. Create a custom mobile app for your business; these are customized smartphone apps that provide engaging information to help promote your product or service.
3. Mobile apps can be a great way to deliver content.

The legwork you put in on the mobile social networks will develop a following; people will talk about your products and services to their friends, and your brand will grow through word of mouth. Post regular videos and photos of your services. Add a discount coupon from time to time. Your business will continue to grow because you spent a few hours wisely using some social media tools.

Generate Traffic and Build a Following

There is a variety of ways to drive traffic to your website. While some methods are free, others will cost money. Understand both so you can maximize your profits using the best traffic methods for your site.

Monetization with Mobile Social Media

Most businesses know they need to incorporate mobile social media to reach new, existing, and potential customers and to demonstrate business impact, yet many are uncertain about how to go about it. Here are six reasons, among many, to utilize mobile social media as measurable business tools and understand the various possibilities of monetizing them.

1. **Mobile social media-enabled synergies among traditional and digital media marketing activities.**
   Mobile social media can integrate many social networking and mobile services, typically in social engagement, customer service, market research, e-commerce, video and banner, forum advertising, coupons/promotions, LBS, search marketing, and more.

   These capabilities combined make mobile social media a superb marketing tool that allows businesses to reach out to global customers, enabling them to able to track customer's response in real-time, improving service quality and, finally, conversions and realized sales.

2. **Mobile Social Media Advertisement**
   Monetizing online content with ads is frequently practiced and is proven effective for both social media and mobile marketing. Learn to create premium, multichannel, and friendly experiences for mobile users.

Allow the mobile user easy access to your content wherever they might be looking for it (on the web or on-the-go). Find ways that you can deliver these experiences in a way unique to your brand and offering. Push unique experiences, loyalty offers, or access to premium content to get users to justify spending their money on a subscription.

3. **Mobile Social Media Influence Other Channels as an Integrated Marketing Strategy**
   Social channels and mobile channels directly affect search SEO, SMO, mobile, LBS, and email. Marketers will spend more effectively on their campaign, resulting in a better success rate, as they will exploit mobile social media.

   Take advantage of the mobile channel by providing targeted ads based on the user's proximity location, search/browse history, social media usage, and personal preferences.

4. **Mobile Social Media Broadens its Reaches**
   Mobile social media integrates flexible formats, from mobisites, websites, weblogs to even social blogs. They may even reach out further from wikis to podcasts, from games to animation and from photographs to video.

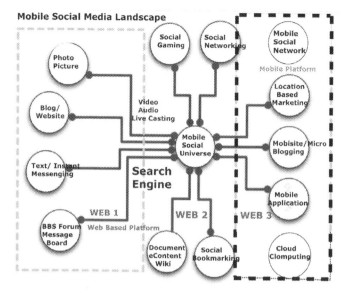

Mobile social media integrate Web 1.0, 2.0, and 3.0

These formats offer marketers monetizing methods through direct or indirect ways, which reach out to customers and from their marketing efforts as well.

Consider the many different types of mobile social media that can serve different industries:

- Mobile-enabled marketing
- Blogs and microblogs
- Forum communities
- Social networking sites
- Virtual game worlds
- Videos and podcast or webcasting
- Virtual social worlds
- Social location-based services

5. **Boost your Brand with Paid Apps**

   Nowadays, media organizations are offering paid apps to offer a premium subscription experience. Having a free app is a great way to gain readership in your base and access new audiences, but having the option to upgrade to a premium app can be a great source of added revenue.

6. **Mobile Social Media Leverages Demographics and Recommendations among Friends and Peers with Mobile Coupons**

   Marketers are able to utilize different types of analytics in the mobile and social sphere to consistently research the time of day, week, geography, etc. This helps determine optimum user reception in order to ensure which campaign or messages will drive engagement and deliver the greatest revenue impact.

Mobile social media, when properly used and managed, willbuild trust among customers and drive increased revenue for retailers; for brand marketers, it will also build better brand awareness, promoting campaignsorganically with actions by customers and their friends.

T he demand for mobile coupons is growing. The easy access to location and target through location-based technology is one of the most buzzed features of mobile social media, which any marketer ought to take better advantage of. *Where is the nearest store or restaurant? Where can I find good fine dining? Which is the best place to get a new gadget product?*

These are questions askedfrequentlyby consumers, and they can be answered with location-aware technology or even by mobile coupons. By using a QR code or a mobile website URL, marketers can not only increase awareness of their product/ service through following a similar mobile coupon example, but also drive consumers to visit a store immediately.

**STEP 1—Attracted by the 25 % Discount,
Customer Scans QR Code**

Step 2—Customer Lands on a Mobile Web page,
tweets/shares to claim their Bonus Front Door Gift

Driving traffic via mobile coupons is usually delivered using the following strategies.

Mobile coupons are usually sent in the form ofSMS coupons or MMS coupons. As all mobile phones have text messaging capability, the text concept offers better penetration and redemption rate;ion addition, it can include landing pages site links with coupon codes toincrease effectiveness.

MMS coupons are usually formatted and delivered right to the inbox of a smart phone. They can be formatted as barcodes or graphics, or presented with a detailed description to allowan informative experience for the recipient.

Create a database of customers' opt-in mobile phone numbers.

To create an effective mobile coupon campaign, it is essential to establish a good database of customers as a permission-based list, who have explicitly opted-in to receive your mobile coupons or deals from the retailer or merchant.

Also setup and promote the campaign through your social networking sites and make sure your mobile-friendly coupons will reach customers' mobile internet enabled device effectively. Format your third screen with an easy to claim redemption instruction for customers to easily to redeem at point of sale or during online shopping. Make sure your staff is aware of the mobile coupon offer and know how to verify validity.

E-commerce and internet payment merchants such as PayPal or Square have recently integrated mobile coupon redemption

API functions with services to validate unique mobile codes during mobile payment checkout. These unique codes can be integrated into most mobile marketing platform to have them distributed as text message coupons or MMS coupons. These can work easily with devices to process debit and credit card payment transactions. Such innovation in eCommerce will allow mobile devices to be used to pay over-the-counter, and even upgrade some tablets or iPhonesto cash register unit as credit card processors.

Mobile Social Media is Monetizable and Measurable

For most business, the goal is to adopt the digital-marketing solutions that can measure both social-media and mobile media efforts for data feedback, like number of visitors, traffic, sharing or viral activities, commentaries, duration of engagement and visits, backlinks, conversions, etc. It is also important to find solutions that can dig deeper into metrics on performance of blog integration, widget activity, social voting, sharing, and bookmarking.

Tracked results provide an overview of performance for marketers to understand (and demonstrate) that their efforts in both social media and mobile marketing can be transformed into social and mobile commerce. The impact on the bottom line can be measured with ease. They can then proceed to make it an integral element of their e-commerce and marketing strategies.

With the advent of eCommerce, business models across the world continue to change drastically. The United Kingdom has the biggest eCommerce market in the world when measured by the amount spent per capita.

China's eCommerce presence continues to expand. China's online shopping sales rose to $42.6 billion in 2010, with 410 million internet users.

eCommerce in mobile social media represents a range of transactions that are distinguished according to the participants.

- Business-to-business (B2B)
- Business-to-consumer (B2C)
- Business-to-employee (B2E)
- Business-to-government(B2G) (aka Business to administration [B2A])
- Business-to-machines (B2M)
- Business-to-manager (B2M)
- Consumer-to-business (C2B)
- Consumer-to-consumer (C2C)
- Citizen-to-government (aka Consumer to Administration [C2A])
- Government-to-business (G2B)
- Government-to-citizen (G2C)
- Government-to-employee (G2E)
- Government-to-government (G2G)
- Manager-to-consumer (M2C)
- Peer-to-peer (P2P)

The E-Shopping Fun Factor

Consumers are more likely to buy when they are having fun. That is the theory behind the merging of eCommerce and entertainment for many retailers, and the entertainment is the main factor that will help their brands stand out.

With a wealth of information at their fingertips, consumers are savvier than ever. They are also much less likely to be swayed by traditional advertising and commercials. They want to be entertained and engaged by marketers.

For decades, the live shows of home shopping channels have demonstrated the power of interaction with consumers; eCommerce businesses are seeking ways to replicate that experience online. Present a product and the people who make it and let consumers interact with them. The key is engagement, and with engagement comes loyalty, which in turn will lead to increased sales.

The World of Mobile Social Media + eCommerce

Mobile social media is growing rapidly given the recent explosion of mobile internet-enabled devices, coupled with consumers' desire (and expectation) for easy access and convenience. Mobile social commerce is set to be the leading emerging technology in today's internet and mobile world. With mobile social media's effectiveness in "search" marketing, consumers prefer to look for ratings and reviews of products or services before making decision on purchases. Their first choice of product information is usually product blogs for reviews and ratings.

More ecommerce merchants have started to offer social mobile commerce solutions geared to small business and startup requirements and budgets. These social mobile customized solutions will let vendors accept payments on a mobile device, and send or text invoices via email to the customers. Mobile carriers, credit card companies, and software companies are all introducing mobile commerce solutions. Therefore, businesses will need to understand the latest market trends for strategic planning of overall ecommerce strategy. Mobile and social commerce are clearly increasing in importance, and particularly concerning how they drive word-of-mouth transactions and in-store traffic.

Always research and determine the specific trends for your own segment of ecommerce to suit your business and find out how your consumers are using mobile and social media as part of their e-shopping fun. Businesses will need to get savvier about integrating e-commerce opportunities into their mobile and social networking account where they are likely to "engage" their customers or potential customers.

It will be worth investing the time understand these trends and consumer behavior while working out your social and mobile commerce strategy.

The Basics of Mobile eCommerce

There are certain essential elements to conducting eCommerce:

- Allocate a place to sell the product, usually a website, Blog, or mobile site.

- Find ways to get traffic to visit your site.
- Find ways to accept online orders.
- Use a payment method through a payment gateway.
- Use a method to fulfill the order, such as shipping products to customers. For software and information, fulfillment can occur with a file download mechanism.
- Develop a way to accept returns.
- Develop a way to handle warranty claims
- Develop a method to provide customer service

Like any other form of marketing, social commerce requires a fully integrated marketing plan.

Encourage shoppers to share your product feature by word of mouth through the SNS and also via email. Use call to action and promotion codes with links thatgo back to your social commerce landing page.

Progressively participate where the conversation is happening, be it on Mobile or social networking site.

This requires training your employees to listen and engage with prospects and customers on your website, third-party sites, and social media. Train your employees who know your product and brand to respond to issues such as negative comments on your social networking site.

Using QR codes as part of your mobile social media marketing program would enable consumers to easily scan your products. This allows them to retrieve your specific product informationor directly link to your page for payment.

Providing the option to track the number of customer service inquiries and responses is of the utmost importance for social commerce.

The main objective is to get the marketers and customers to be engaged on the social media platforms where your prospects and customers are provided with the information they need. Whether it is on your website, mobisite, or social media networks, customers should be able to access for purchase as well.

Here are three main methods that marketers follow to incorporate eCommerce as part of their social and mobile commerce sites:

1. Lower transaction costs—if an eCommerce site is implemented well, the web can significantly help to lower costs by automated processes.
2. Larger purchases per transaction—If marketers offer an add-on option so customers can consider "what other people who ordered this product also purchased," customers are likely to buy more than they might buy at a normal store.
3. Integration into the business cycle—awebsite that is well-integrated into the business cycle can offer customers more information than previously available, such as order tracking.

With new technology, mobile commerce solutions come with automated tools making it possible to interact with consumers in multiple ways at virtually no cost. Small businesses and individuals benefit greatly from the reduced cost to create the eCommerce website, take the orders, and accept the payment through automated systems.

Considerations When Building a Mobile eCommerce Site for Social Networking or Mobile Website

There are things you need to consider when building an eCommerce site:

- **Suppliers**—Without manufacturer or developer support, you may not be able to offer products, so checkout the suppliers to determine the quality of their product and services.
- **Price point**—Price comparisons are extremely easy for the consumer, so your price is very important in a transparent market.
- **Customer relations**—Integrate features such as E-mail, FAQs, knowledge bases, forums, and chat rooms into your eCommerce site to help differentiate yourself from the competition.
- **Remember the back end of the ordering process**—fulfillment, returns, customer service. These processes will make or break any retail business.
- **SNS and mobile ecommerce sites**—these are usually independent, but the tools you need for mobile optimization are unique.
- **Smartphone popularity**—every business needs a fast, easy-to-use mobile commerce site. Customize your mobile website for smaller screens and clearer images. Create shorter pages with streamlined navigational

options. Make sure your brand and layout is consistent between your online website and mobile site, to build familiarity with your customers.

- **For clicking**—a Facebook post, tweet, a mobile ad, a QR code, another SMS ads, or an email, the mobile

It is important to remember that you will not sell products that mobile shoppers cannot see. You need make sure they can easily find what they are looking for and that the images clearly show what it is that they are buying. Make sure your brand and layout is consistent between your online website and mobile site to build familiarity with your customers.

CHAPTER 10

Get your Business and Brand to Go Mobile

Consumers spend an average of 30 seconds interacting with advertisements; compared to an average of just spending 11 seconds visiting websites or a sales page. In addition to spending more time on advertisements, 35 of every 1,000 consumers were more likely to click to learn more about advertisements. This is in comparison to an average of just 1 in 1,000 that would click through from a sales page.

Brands have realized the importance of advertisements and are building a large presence with social media networks. The technology is referred to as a "cloud-based ad platform" because it infuses advertisements with live content from sites including Facebook, Renren and Twitter.

Some media and technology companies, such as Kontera, are taking a similar approach with in-text advertising. This is where advertisers pay for keywords to be hyperlinked within an article or blog post. Instead of leaving the advertisement page, when a user clicks on the words; the new technology enables a pop-up window on the same page. Many of these advertisements are still emphasizing on their brands over their products.

Positioning the cursor over those words causes an advertisement to pop-up in a window, promoting things like, sweepstakes. Highlighted posts of the Brands, on Facebook page, gives details about contests.

Mobile Apps and Branding

With mobile and social media booming in the internet, advertisers are now thinking and investing their money in online advertisements to capture their audiences in the social media landscape. The technology which is driving brand engagement or effective performance marketing on the social graph is increasing each day.

For the social web, consumers are quite easily influenced by their friends' opinions and social media is not only able to effectively display an advertisement to a user; but also capable of displaying in their SNS to friends who are interested in that advertisement or brand as well. This provides engagement and click-through rates on social advertisements will dramatically increase.

With iPhone being so popular and new android smartphone models coming into the market rapidly, mobile app stores are carrying an increasingly wide range of mobile apps. It has been reported that above 13 billion apps have been downloaded, in November 2011. For many consumers, apps are becoming the most popular means to use the internet, whether for games, watch videos, read ebooks, Mapping, email or other uses.

Mobile apps have managed to boost sales for major brands besides mobile social networking services. Both will play a major role in complementing the overall mobile social media brand marketing strategy.

Mobile Apps therefore provide brands with a ready source of income and also a rich media experience to the user of the brand.

Advertising and Branding has therefore begun to shift and advertisers who own major brands are investing in mobile social media platform in a big way. The recent acquisition by Google for AbMob and Apple's for iAd network are proof of the true power of mobile applications in the context.

Marketers should also start to appreciate the value of mobile app technology and is becoming increasingly important to know how to make your app stand out in its application and turn them into effective marketingtools.

Prior to designing your mobile apps;

The priority is to fully understand, each mobile phone's platform i.e. Apple iOS or Google Androids. They have specific user interface and design guideline for specific devices. Failure to do so will create incompatibly problems or issues which will deem failure for aggregation to various App store.

When developing your mobile app, marketers should consider the following, especially when designing on this function and application;

iPaddisplaying Different Mobile Apps

- **Functionality Of App**

Keep it simple by placing focus on the core functions and activities that mobile users will require. For example, go for less functions but use a simple user interface that users can easily understand and is screen friendly. You should also do some market research, to figure out your targeted market and if the features are for your desktop application or website. Consider on the interaction requirements like mobile friendliness and ease of use to ensure minimal navigation and easy access. Branding is done by including your products' images, which makes it screen friendly and make it applicable on different devices also. Consider how it can enhance your your business and be appreciated by consumers.

- **Appealing Look**

Mobile apps that are appealing in design or provide entertainment, like games or a nice friendly animations, helpsinspire users to share it with others which could benefit your business greatly (due to the extra exposure). To be able to instantly connect to a broader customer base is one of the powerful benefits of creating an app for your business.

- **Frequent updates**

Easy updating features must be incorporated in your mobile app as it gives your business a convenient and trendy way to stay connected with customers. It can be used to show that your business is keeping up with the latest trends. Through frequent updates, latest information that will benefit the user will be easilyavailable for them, providing a good after-sales service.

- **Users on the Go**

Furthermore, you must understand how users would prefer to use mobile devices and applications. They are called mobile devices, giving the concept "on-the-Go". Users like it fast and simple to access, so that they can complete a task and proceed on to other businesses.

How the user interacts with the mobile application in their palm and fingers is another important interaction tool you must consider. The finger serves as a pointing device and requires reactive touchscreen technologies to work properly with the surface area when it contacts. So interactive elements, such as buttons or navigation positions and layouts of other elements have to be considered with proper spacing. This is to ensure that the finger can hit on the right elements for its intended function.

- **Fast Download**

Build apps that are easy and fast to download. Remember to build your apps based on the profile or demographics of your audience. This is important in terms of how an app appeals and looks as younger readers are prone to nice-looking icons or graphics. It must be all for the readers' experience.

- **Marketing Apps Via Social Networking services**

Upon completion of your apps, it will be necessary to test the functions and usability of the application, before uploading to major appstores or at your mobile social media site. Conducting a usability testing throughout the development stages will help to ensure that the final end design will satisfy consumers and also save the company from costly redevelopment efforts.

Even so, marketers will still need to work out methods to effectively implement apps into their framework, so as to fit into their mobile marketing strategy.

Due to the much wider choice of both apps and brands, consumers are no longer limited to the Android Smartphone or iPhone. Nokia Symbian is promising their users with more and more features and functions. There are hundreds of different platforms where marketers can upload their apps for even specific application related to their apps profile.

Before readers can gain access to your app, they first need to know that it actually exists. With so many apps available now and so few ways to promote them within app stores themselves, this is a relatively difficult task to accomplish and it is completely irrespective of content quality.

Most appstores, wanting to be fair to all developers, will leave the promotion of their apps to themselves. Your marketing efforts therefore need to be focused on driving readers directly to your app's link in your appstore.

The following provides some tips to push readers to your apps through Mobile social media:

Placing a mobile advertisement within other appson mobile Websites. This will cause a Viral effect, but different marketing and promotional strategies are required for the various application platform

- Featuring the application in customer communications should be frequently organized. Link your mobile apps on your Website and blog. Mention it in your direct mail or mobile SMS to customers and send a promotional email to your e-mail list
- The mobile device is always switched on. The marketer can effectively exploit on this channel to market further. Some marketers sponsor and give apps for free and use it as a viral marketing tool on the mobile social networking platform. This will include links to your appstore
- Consider using the social networks to introduce the mobile apps through fanpages and analyze customer preferences and behaviour whenever they signup. SNS is able to provide customers demographic data when they are online and marketer can then use this data to offer highly personalized service to his customers
- Cross promote your mobile branding apps initiatives on social media by posting a keyword and short code of your mobile apps to your wall.

Branding with Mobile Apps for business

Mobile marketing is the new effective marketing platform for every business. Most businesses are looking for ways to reduce their marketing costs and to generate consistent business sales to maintain their business. There are many social mobile tools available which is suited for different business requirements.

Thanks to iBuildapps, iPhone's Appmaker and Google's App Inventor; these websites provide simple to make wizard programs for producing your own personal or Business app that can be used for your mobile marketing purpose.

Using mobile apps in your mobile marketing campaign will able to give you an insight of consumer's behaviour. It is done in real time. This information will be helpful to the marketer, as it will help him to constantly improve on his campaign strategies. Below are a few cases of how a mobile application could have the most benefit for a business:

- E-commerce application—one of the most effective uses of mobile apps is for mobile commerce opportunities—a successful mobile application will essentially pay for itself over time.

- SNS marketing—Such apps can be integrated into your mobile social media platform providing an engaging experience for the app user directly from their smartphone, they also allow marketers to share their products and services information with their SNS network, affording greater brand visibility.

- Mobile advertisement—One of the major key benefits of the mobile application platform is that it can be monetized through advertising. Third party mobile ads can be integrated to the Mobile application to generate monetary gain.

Considering the immense amount of interest that is being generated with regard to the use of Mobile social media as promotional tools, businesses both big and small seem to be making a beeline for them. However, not everyone succeeds at social media based promotional campaigns. Here are some simple pointers to help you leverage your promotional campaign using social media:

- **Determine Your Goals**—Do not put the cart before the horse. Although you can set up a free business page on both Facebook and Renren and have it up and running in just a few minutes, you need to have set it up with pertinent goals in mind. Setting up a Facebook Fan page would allow you to promote the business and build a following even before you launch.

- **Engage and Interact with Your Fans**—Use mobile social media to interact and build a relationship with your fans and engage them in the 'happenings' on your fan page. A store may use its RenRen or Facebook page to pose a question of the day, promote contests or start discussions on items of interest. Mobile Social media empowers with enhances features like location based services with geolocation mapping, images, story boards, discussions, groups, QR codes, mobile apps are some of the common tools that can ensure success to your campaign

- **Don'tCompromise on Content**—If you create high quality, original content you will always draw the attention of people. They will appreciate you for investing your time and be more loyal to your venture. Promote your brand along with your products or services, but not in every posting. People may really be interested in how your product or service can help them to solve a problem but you'll turn them off if you are pushy and tend to shove them advertisement all the time. They like to get to know you as someone who is helpful and will look to you for advice or referrals. Building your personal brand is not on the priority list for this blog but by being helpful, you will promote and build your Brand.

*   **Build Contacts**—Networking with people to create a group can help, support, comment, criticize and offer suggestions for one another. This is very important.

Readers will "like" your status on Facebook or "retweet" your tweets on Twitter only when you build a relationship with them. Do not underestimate the people power that social media can get for you but instead, capitalize on it and work your way to the top.

What are Mobile Social Networking Sites or services?

Mobile social networking sites are huge online databases where users of similar interest, converse and connect with one another using both mobile devices and their desktop computer.

They initially form a smaller lesser known faction of the major social networking sites like major powerhouses namely facebook, twitter, Weibo and many others but with the fast development of Mobile devices like smartphones, it has brought together the integration of web based and mobile based social networking sites to complete the mobile social media umbrella as both occurs in Virtual communities.

Mobile social networking sites usually are mobile portals of an already successful site like Facebook or SinaWeibo. They offer a wider series of functions, including chatrooms, photo sharing, instant messaging, location based services and customizable web-pages. Many of them also offer inexpensive international phone calls and SMS for the price wary.

A recent survey report that social networking is one of the primary ways mobile users communicate with each other, and is one of the most significant drivers of internet usage on mobile devices.

Since then while mobile web migrated from featured mobile technologies to full mobile access to the internet especially through smartphone which can served addition functions like sharing photo, located based services, playing multimedia product, mobile communication or utilize the global position services capability. These are facilitated by new advances in combination of technology in Web 2.0 and Web 3.0 with advances in hardware and software which extend further development in technologies like in location based services, Web 3.0 and cloud computing for mobile social media.

Mobile social networking sites used for business will usually focused on exchanging information for business opportunities, employees recruitment, new business ventures, job inquiries, product introduction, business deals, business promotion and more.

Sites including LinkedIn, Foursquare, Facebook, Flickr, Yahoo, RenRen, Weibo, Mocospace and an ever-expanding list of others fall into the professional networking arena.

CHAPTER 11

The Ever—Changing Landscape of Mobile Social Networks with Location-Based Marketing

Providing a useful list of important business-oriented mobile social networking sites is a constant challenge. Newly developed sites arrive with a buzz, while older ones may disappear from the web. Other, newer featured sites expand their offerings to adapt to the mobile social network.

Check out the following important mobile social networking sites with both web-based and mobile platforms. These are the most famous sites based on their popularity, membership size, and broad range of features. These sites were all functioning smoothly and successfully at the time of this writing. Several of them are so large and well established that they are not likely to dissolve any time soon.

The various mentioned networking sites differ from one another in significant ways. Their differences include their size of membership; country of origin; geographic location of members; rules for connecting; and advanced features beyond the basic posting of a profile. However, how marketers utilize them for their marketing agendas will make a difference as well.

Consumer adoption is steadily increasing, and mobile-specific features such as check-ins are being incorporated with location-based services. Mobile social networking presents significant marketing opportunities for brands seeking to engage an audience in contexts and environments where this was previously not possible.

Mobile social networking is set to get bigger and better as new startups, small business, and major corporations compete in the space to bring better and more innovative solutions to consumers. The opportunity for brands is always growing, especially when newer technology keep developing.

When developing mobile social network campaigns, brands need to recognize the difference between the mindset of people who are accessing their social network via their mobile versus those accessing through their PC. They need to frame their offerings accordingly. The following will discuss on some of the more trending sites with high volume of members using both web and mobile platforms.

Major Leading Mobile Social Networking sites

Facebook
Facebook has more traffic than any other social networking system on the web, with over 500 billion page views every month. Facebook is simple to use and fast. If you set up your page right,

you will be able to get killer traffic in just a few hours. In order to achieve that kind of traffic, here are some steps which you might want to follow:

1. **Use Fan Pages**

   Although groups will help you interact with followers, not everyone will be able to join a group. So, consider to integrate a Brand using Fan Pages in order to leverage Facebook's viral capabilities. Groups are unofficial and can be created by any user. Fan Pages can only be created by official representatives, and applications can be added. Posts made by a Brand through their Fan Pages are included in a Fan's newsfeeds. A Fan Page basically operates like a profile for an organization or business

2. **Show Personality on your Fan Page**

   If you are trying to create a connection, remember that machines do not require personality, but fans enjoy interacting with someone who has one. When making your posts, make sure to include fun updates and other contents that your fans might enjoy and that will encourage more engagement.

3. **Tag Liberally and Often**

   People love to look at photos. Take as many pictures as you can at events and post them to your Facebook pages. Tag as many people as you can in the photos and then invite your fans to tag people in the photos. Tagging notifies not only those who have been tagged, but also their friends. Thus, this will draw more traffic to your fan page because the friends will want to see.

4. **Incorporate videos**

   Groups posting videos on their fan pages can generate more
   interaction and message postings. Posted messages due to
   the setup of Facebook are then shared with others, adding
   to the viral effect.

5. **Incorporate Facebook into your events**

   If you have a special event planned, be sure to invite your
   Facebook fans to the party. Post the date of the event
   well in advance to promote it. Let all of your followers on
   Facebook know, so that they can tell all of their friends and
   invite them to your event. Facebook is the largest social
   media network and the best place to advertise in social
   media today. With over 750 million users, it is the most well
   developed advertising platform of all the social networks.
   Ads on Facebook are still cheap, so it makes a great place to
   advertise. Other online programs like Google AdWords will
   cost you significantly more.

   Develop a fan page on Facebook and then pay to advertise
   that fan page to gain "likes." This will not only help you make
   a presence, but you will also be creating your own network
   of targeted fans on Facebook you can then communicate
   with.

   Facebook can be accessed through mobile web browser. Its
   business Facebook page can be used to add friends, put up
   pages of campaigns and provide a phonebook for all your
   contacts. This application is therefore able to help users
   virtually get connected to almost everywhere.

RENREN

RenRen, in Chinese, means *People to People*; this is sometimes also known as the "Everyone's network" in China.

RenRen is one of the leading social networking sites in China, with an IPO in the US. RenRen includes a wireless application version for users on mobile devices. An instant messaging service is also available; it is similar to Facebook chat. RenRen has recently launched its co-branded credit card holders, with location-based services, which allows customers to check-in from their current location to receive promotional treats and loyalty incentives found nearby.

RenRen provides a user interface quite similar to the old facebook model but is very suitable for marketers to set up fanpages on its site. Their format was more focused on real people connecting using RenRen to get friend to connect with old friends to increase membership profile.

It has a few unique features: it tracks and provides brief footprints of who last visited your page and allows third party developers to develop games for RenRen. It already has a great set of games due to its open platform, but continues to focus on in-house gaming efforts. With a stronger focus on social games, this is popular with different countries in Asia. This popularity has created a niche that suits younger web surfers aged between 18-25, unlike other SNSs. RenRen is strict about brand accounts, and there is a daily cap on the number brand accounts that can be opened each day. All applications must be by form submission and be approved by RenRen only.

With its interface format similar to Facebook, marketers can actively participate with developing advertisements, games, and eCommerce-related products to generate new revenue sources. However, if engaging in this, it is important to be careful of censorship practices in China.

TWITTER

Twitter is a social networking website that you can use to start generating site traffic and is a great advertising platform for your product. This social networking service is formatted as a microblogging site in terms of its functionality, and posts are limited to 140-charactersor less.

The key to tweet marketing is to follow other tweeters and to get followers to follow you. When you have thousands of users following you, you can advertise your products though Twitter and everyone who follows you will get your advertisements. With its fast tweeting features, users can tweet on the latest news and create a trend. The "trending Craze" is usually based on user-shared content; this attracts major news agencies, who use Twitter to see what people are talking about.

Even though Twitter is huge and has grown at an unprecedented rate in its five years of operation, it has the least-developed advertising platform of any of the social media networks. On Twitter you can buy a sponsored tweet or pay to promote a trend on the main page for advertising.

In order to be successful on Twitter, you will have to manually build up your network of followers and you will have to determine which ones are the right people to follow you in order to make your presence more noticeable.

If you work at it and achieve Twitter success, you will be rewarded with the "snowball effect". After you post a tweet, your followers will re-tweet, and the followers of your followers will re-tweet, and so on and on.

Another advantage to people tweeting about you is the increase in your SEO. Someone searching for a topic you tweeted about will find your business if you get people tweeting about it. By getting the "snowball" rolling with an initial tweet, your followers are putting the message fully into the public view on the search engines.

Combining that with automatic updates to your Facebook Fan Page (which is focused on a targeted group of followers and marketers), you can achieve a broad network reaching out to people and their friends. Twitter also utilizes mobile technology with the Twitter Location tool, which is compatible with third party geolocation technology, enabling pointing to locations tweet with a nearby address.

KAIXIN

Chinese social networking sites operator Oak Pacific Interactive has announced that it will gradually integrate its two social networking sites, Renren.com and Kaixin.com after October 2011.

Kaixin001 was able to attract office workers, who are the savviest and the most monetizable demographics of social network users in China. The combination of both SNSs will push the development of Chinese SNS websites to a new scale and height. According to industry watchers, the integration of the two websites will make the growth of other SNS competitive, and new developments will be expected.

SINA WEIBO

SinaWeibo has been a microblogging site since it started. It has gradually evolved into an almost fully-fledged SNS. It started from the basics in social networking: content creation, through enriched multi-media posts (tweets), which even allowed users to post pictures and videos and accelerated down the path of building a social network with almost daily updates.

Microblogs allow followers to follow one another, though usually they may not know each other. Weibo makes it easier and allows users' friends to recommend friends. It can also post pictures and videos, and it even provides public pages (like Fan pages) that are customizable, where users can directly share their pictures and videos using their mobile devices. With such functions, Weibo has also integrated social location services, called Micro-Locations (微领地—Wei Ling Di), into its renewed platform with instant messaging and a voicemail option.

With additional features for open platforms in its application, Weibo commands an advantage over other SNS and leads the market as an open platform for developers in Apps and gaming software, and even cloud computing applications. This allows a full range of possibilities to be introduced into the Weibo platform, where special applications like social commerce, centralized messaging system, interactive advertisement, and virtual games with currency and monetization programs. These features attract marketers to participate with the site to promote their products and services online.

Weibo tends to have a higher entertainment value and its trend function shows popular tags categorized into various topics, which has found a niche with celebrities, where famous actors and actress maintain their blogs at SinaWeibo to build their number of fans in the major Chinese market. Its demographic reflects more focus on reaching out to younger generations, aged from 17-36. As Weibo has both Chinese and English sites, the marketing implication will be wider as users prefer to use SNSs that provide multiple applications and services to simplify their mobile social experiences with easy, frequent updatesand gaming aimed at relaxation combined with social sharing.

QZONE (Tencent)

Tencent has two social networking sites called Qzone and Pengyou, which, combined, had over 468 million users as of March 2011. The difference between Qzone and Pengyou is clear: Qzone is a social network of qq instant messaging friends; while Pengyou is a network of friends in real life. The former is quite new and is still in its beta version at the time of writing.

Qzone has over 500 Million active users covering Asian countries from Singapore to China. Its QQ messenger services took Asia by storm when they were introduced in 2005, just when MSN was the leading instant messaging service in the world. QQ has been popular, especially with the Chinese educated, and Asia has many in this demographic. They find that QQ allows them to communicate easily with its Chinese character software. In

Qzone, users can write blogs, share favorite photos and pictures, listen to the MP3 songs, and express their moods with their cute avatars and unique characters.

Qzone also provides advanced functions so that the customers who are good at creating web pages can customize Qzone and add-ons with different skins and ornaments to distinguish themselves from others. It allows interaction between users with their own Qzone. However, most services provided by Qzone are not free; members usually resort to buying the "Canary Diamond" (cost 10 Yuan per Month)to access to such services like Tencent'sinternet services, QQ Messenger, QQ Show, QQ Games, QQ Pet, and Qzone.

Qzone is a closed platform and is not too accessible, but their popularity has brought them in line with other social networking sites. For marketers, the main draw is their comparatively young and rural users that pay Qzone so they can play the games online with their friends. Their business strategy is to encroach mainly on the demographics of teens. Qzone may bring forth good monetization opportunities for Asian media.

YouTube
YouTube is an online public communications site and is intertwined with the social media networks. Registered users are allowed to upload their videos for viewing and have access available for the public. Anyone can view videos posted on YouTube. Videos range from beginner to professional videos.

You can put just about anything you want on the YouTube site, and you will find just about anything to watch on YouTube. Most of the videos on YouTube will never be seen anywhere else, regardless of how interesting or entertaining they may be.

YouTube is a great tool for promoting your product for little cost. If you are looking for cheap ways of advertising, this is the way to go. People love to watch videos.

Sometimes it is tough to get a start in some areas by yourself these days. For instance, it is difficult at best to break into the music industry, but this is a way to showcase your music for the public. You can put your video on YouTube for little to no cost. Once it is online, people who like your music will share the video with friends. Who knows how far you can go . . . but regardless of your level of success, it is another way to promote a product or idea with next to no cost.

It is a no-brainer. Why would you not use such a valuable tool in marketing? Uploading and downloading is easy and relatively fast, depending on your connection to the Internet. Come up with an idea, a catchy title, and start filming!

YOUKU

Youku is one of China's most popular video streaming services. It focuses on maintaining steady and smooth streaming for consumers, which they may not always be able to receive from YouTube, and the streaming service is presently utilized by major brands, especially from the fashion industry.

Like YouTube, you can do anything you want with your video—embed it on your website, email it to your friends, or simply be content with the knowledge that your video is now hosted on servers in China. Youku popularity has been enhanced due to their agreement with hundreds of major media partners around the world, who have been broadcasting dramas and movies for on-demand purpose. This attracts web surfers to visit their sites and utilize their videos.

Youku states that they offer a safe environment for advertisers and has so far generated advertising revenue from over 250 companies to date, including Louis Vuitton, Pepsi, Nike, Adidas, L'Oréal, IBM, Microsoft, Google, Samsung, Nokia, Mercedes-Benz, BMW, etc.

The company also earns search advertising revenue through partnerships with search giants Baidu and Google. The company recently launched its 3G mobile subscription version of Youku, and also a video e-commerce partnership with Taobao, the eBay of China. An important niche of Youku is their strategic plan to provide TV-like, cross-media, and internet marketing solutions to advertiser clients that are growing rapidly.

Youku's main advantage for marketers is mainly due to their Mandatory ads, which are usually played prior to the actual video being played. The brief mandatory ads are an effective ways to reach targeted groups of audience, as such adscan be played on selected shows that appeal to the target audience.

LinkedIn

LinkedIn is a business-related social networking site for professionals, also known as B2B, founded in December 2002 and launched in May 2003. LinkedIn reported more than 120 million registered users by spring of 2011 in more than 200 countries and territories globally. In June 2011, LinkedIn had 33.9 million unique visitors: an increase of 63 percent from a year earlier.

Individuals who use LinkedIn are self-employed (80%) and small business owners (78%), outnumbering large businesses or corporations (71%). LinkedIn projects the number of self-employed are the most likely to increase their use of the site in 2011 (68% versus 61% for all other types of marketers).

Features of the network include:
Registered users can maintain a list of contact details for people with whom they have some level of relationship. Users can invite anyone at any time (whether a site user or not) to become a connection.

The LinkedIn community is supported with a wide range of social media tools. There are many benefits to maintaining such a list of contacts. This list can be used in various ways:

- Marketers can build a contact network consisting of their direct connections, the connections of each of their connections, and the connections of second-degree connections. These can be used to gain an introduction to someone a person wishes to know through a mutual contact.
- A connection can be used to find jobs, people, and business opportunities recommended by somebody.
- Employers can list jobs and search for potential candidates through their connections.

- Job seekers can review a profile of hiring managers to discover if an existing contact can introduce them.
- Users can post photos or import their blogs and power point presentations directly on their profile.
- Users can follow different companies to get notifications about new jobs and offers available.
- There are tens of thousands of groups on LinkedIn, ranging from Hobbyist to Automotive professional, and targeting them for specific services to build up relationships. Posting links to your blog or website can help to engage fellow members for product promotion or discussion.

Marketers interested in specific companies can research them on LinkedIn. Statistics regarding the company are provided when a user performs a search.

All of this information is designed to help the users make more informed choices or decisions. For a business owner, the site offers a profile of a pool of potential prospects.

For marketers who spend a lot of time on the go, they can also access LinkedIn Mobile, which can be used anywhere, at m.linkedin.com.

LinkedIn mobile features include searching and viewing profiles, inviting new connections, access to LinkedIn answers, actionable network updates (i.e. LinkedIn Mobile optimized for iPhone), and is also available for Blackberry and any other Internet enable phone. It is currently available in multiple languages (English,

French, German, Spanish, Japanese, and Chinese), with additional languages to follow.

Foursquare

Launched in 2009, Foursquare is a geolocation social media mobile platform that makes specific physical locations easier to locate using GPS. Users can check-in via a smartphone app or SMS to share their current location with friends while collecting gaming points and virtual badges. This is a useful mobile social media networking service for restaurant, shopping mall, and shop owners. Foursquare canaward the badge of the "Mayor," a designation given to someone who frequents a location the most. A company can also create special badges that convert to discounts and freebies to non-mayors who frequent a particular establishment. In this way, customerscan access discounts while business owners can bring in more customers.

Foursquare can be integrated with both Facebook and Twitter. Users can also post their location to these networks for their members to see. Foursquare itself has a similar "Business page" function, where brands can recommend venues and activities, and customers can follow a page to see tips that have been posted, or click on your links which you have placed that align with your products or services.

Foursquare enables brands to connect with their market even without a physical location. As Foursquare continues to leverage mobile technology, it attracts mostly young people and travelers, who prefer to share locations with their business associates and friends.

Jiepang

With the rise of mobile internet usage and mobile social networks growing at a most exponential pace, marketers focused on specific geographic location with location-based service can eventually become a massive revenue generator. Jiepang is one of China's most popular location-based services and is driven by the gaming component model similar to Foursquare.

Jiepang attracts mostly young people and travelers who share certain location with their friends. Main advertisers will offer coupons, discounts, and special deals to those that check in at their business. In China, rich yuppies who trend athigh fashion retailers make use of Jiepang's badge on their profile to show their status. This trend set off a marketing success, as peers and friends will like their contacts to know that they frequent such high fashion places to gain their status reputation.

Like other popular mobile social networks, Jiepang focuses on major brands and enrolled celebrities support to attract users. By allowing users to check-in to follow favorite brands, this strategy has been able to attract users to their location-based services.

Another effective strategy used by Jiepang users is to connect with other users who check into competitors' or targeted business. An owner of a restaurant always competing with a nearby Pizza business could connect those customers who visit the Pizza business to attract and migrate their customers from their location to his account.

This method is usually practiced by small businesses, and Jiepang users will usually link their post update or message to RenRen or SinaWeibo accounts so that each update can be synced to all compatible mobile social networks.

$$* \quad * \quad *$$

Mobile social networking is where individuals converse, connect, and share, using their smartphones, just as we have web-based social networking sites like Facebook, Bebo, Myspace and many more on PCs. Growing faster than the PC internet, mobile social networking technology is just not limited to SMS and MMS, but is continuously revolutionizing towards sophisticated interactions of internet virtual communities.

Japan, Korea, and China are the highest user of the mobile social networking, even compared to western countries. In Japan, besides 80% of users of 3G network participating, there are numerous other mobile SNSs penetrating into the existing market. Prior to the latest easily-accessible technologies (like mobile browsers, mobile communication, location-based services, augmented reality services, and smart phones apps), companies had to depend on other methods to attract users as they did not have such wireless phone carriers to distribute mobile social networking technology.

The Evolution of New Mobile Social networking Platforms

Mobile users constitute one of the fastest areas of growth in the social web, where we notice the rise of people who accessed Facebook, LinkedIn, Myspace, Sinaweibo, RenRen, and Twitter. Therefore, it is no surprise that mobile social networks are becoming more and more popular. Even the top non-mobile powerhouse social networking sites that originally started with desktop networking have setup mobile portals.

The effort has since started a new trend where we noticed new major players have also come into the scene with platforms dedicated to the mobile segment of the mobile social media pie.

All of the sites listed below share a certain set of features, which are common to all mobile social networking sites. They allow the user to create a profile, send and receive text messages via phone or computer, and visit an on-line version of the mobile site. Usually, such mobile social networking sites are modeled and offer at least four of the following features:

1) These sites focus on the ability to send short, text-based messages (SMS) to a large number of people at once.

2) These sites will usually provide tagging of particular locations with information and images with location-based services by keeping track of where your contacts are. They also allow you to check if there's anyone near a particular venue or location. They make use of a World mapping option to let the user check the address of a particular tagged location.

3) They provide services for mobile social networking, with functions including multi-media posts, check-in, gaming with coupon campaigns, chatrooms, photo sharing, instant messaging, and Cloud sharing of media files like music.

4) Similar to social networking sites, the trend of e-commerce plays another important role in marketing with mobile technology.

Friendstribe.com

Friendstribe.com is a mobile social network designed with every aspect to be used from your cell phone through text messaging. You can practice mass messaging of your location to your friends, use the "find" command to receive directions to a venue through a text message, and create a group photo gallery with your friends.

BrightKite.com

Brightkite is an effective mobile network, especially for travelers and people attending conferences, exhibitions, and seminars in major cities. It allows for your network of friends to keep track of where others may be at any moment. Users can send updates to the service via text messaging or email, to update their profile with location updates, pictures, and notes. Twitter users are increasingly using the network to update friends with status locations sent to their Twitter streams.

Loopnote.com

Loopnote lets people create alerts. People can subscribe via email, IM, text, or RSS. Loopnote hopes to become more than just a mobile social network by setting its sights on becoming a social compass. By alerting you when your friends are nearby and letting you find out about what is going on near your location, Loopnote hopes to point you in the right social direction.

Treemo.com

Treemo is an online and mobile community dedicated to sharing digital media, empowering self-expression, and transforming creativity into action. By offering an ever-evolving gallery of video, audio, photography, text, and visual art, Treemo inspires visitors to create their own digital expressions, and to share those creations with the world—on the web and on mobile phones.

Groovr.com

Groovr is a mobile network connected not just online, but in real life, too. User can post a picture, message, or video to theirGroovr profiles. Users will be able to meet other users in their neighborhood, check-in, and check out hot new places reviewed by fellow users.

Gypsii

Gypsii is a mobile social network with a theme of recording your life by snapping photos or recording video, geotagging it, and sending it to your friends across the network. Gypsii has mobile clients for a number of smartphones, including Windows Mobile and Blackberry, and an iPhone app is coming down the pipeline soon. In addition to sharing your places with friends on the network, Gypsii is linked in to Facebook and Twitter, making it easier to share your places.

Socialight.com

Socialight lets you create, share, and discover virtual sticky notes stuck to actual places all around you. Sounds simple right? It is! It is also very powerful . . .

Zannel

Zannel is about life in real time. It is a way for you and your friends to share what you are doing, feeling, and seeing as it happens. It is a free service that allows you to create your own mobile page where you can post videos, pictures, and text updates with your phone to instantly share with your friends and start a conversation. You can also follow friends, meet new friends, and watch videos.

ShoZu

Connecting your phone and your online life has never been easier. With ShoZu, you can interact with huge list of sites and communities—from Flickr to Facebook, YouTube to Blogger, the list goes on.

Sifang (a direct translation of Foursquare in Chinese)

It offers a location based service (LBS), where users virtually "check-in" to real locations, sharing data with venue owners and operators as well as their peers. It is partnered mostly with the food & beverage, fashion, and retail sectors, which suits the tastes of its customer base. It has built up a network by synchronizing users' status updates with some of the largest social networking sites, including Kaixin, RenRen, Douban, Windows Live, Google Talk, and Twitter.

Measuring Mobile Social Media Marketing Success

A sound, comprehensive marketing strategy should produce a successful MSM campaign. A campaign must be a particular, systematic course of aggressive activities aimed at accomplishing a specific goal and should be insular and linear with a defined start and end date and a precise goal.

MSM campaigns must be monitored, measured and analyzed so you can tweak your methods or make changes as necessary to ensure optimal success.

In order to measure whether or not your brand's mobile social media campaign is working properly and successful in reaching its goals, you will need to find the right information. This information will help you identify relevant mobile social media activity, estimate its relative value with a benchmark comparison, analyze the relationship between the mobile social media activity and campaign objectives (intended results), and understand the business outcome (achieved results).

There are manyfactors in any business, and online marketers using mobile social media marketing campaigns need to be able to gauge the impact of their mobile social media activities and content accordingly. These factors include (but are not limited to):

- Brand visibility—You must be able to gain the attention of the target audience through brand building via MSM. Frequent posting of quality content will maintain high visibility for your brand.
- User interaction—You want to see site interaction such as the users buying something online, opting in, posting a review, commenting, sharing, or "liking."
- Inbound Links—You want to have other sites or blogs link back to your site to rank higher in the search engines result page.

Website and Mobisite Traffic

You need to monitor the traffic to your website and how often it is shared by a user. The important thing in web site analytics is measuring what worked or didn't against outcomes (downloads, sales, registrations, sharing, etc.);these practices should be emulatedin mobile analytics practice. Data collected could be tied to some effective mobile interaction events:

- check-ins, video view
- sharing (links, image, comments, etc.)
- click-to-call
- coupon redemption at points of sale

Segmentation between Mobile Site and Website

Mobisites or SoLoMo are sometime optimized differently based on operating system between iOS or Android platform for mobile phone and tablets. It is therefore recommended to be categorize into segments to suit the profile. Your treatment of specific data should be explicitly related to the apps conversion result or its screen size, as appropriate.

SoLoMo Activity: The analysis of the mobile social interaction with location-based services should aim to measure and compare the social activity in response to video, click-to-call, check-in, coupon redemption exercise against leveraging location data. The purpose of this comparison is to learn and build better a business strategy around location venues like restaurants, stores, and services. Factors to consider in comparing mobile platforms include operating system, its mobility, and brand acceptance unique to different users preference.

Social   Locations   Mobile

Monitoring the Buzz

Mobile Social media monitoring may also be referred to as buzz monitoring or blog mining. This is the process of tuning in to your mobile social media and making sure you note what you observe and record specific online conversations that are relevant to your business and its brand.

Businesses will need to monitor their site visibility in order to maintain their reputation. You are not the only one online, so you should also monitor your employees, your competition, and your industry. Make sure to monitor targeted sales and promotional campaigns.

The requirement to establish web analytics will provide marketers useful information such as time spent on sites and specific pages, and time spent using mobile apps to make data-driven decisions and establish consumer behavior patterns based on their interactions within their mobile social media site.

This allows the marketer to optimize site design, and improve site navigation and usability from their established mobile metrics, a marketer needs to analyze strategy based on metrics on campaigns results, traffic, conversion rate, mobile efforts, and keywords tracking.

Finding the answers to these questions will lead to effective marketing for marketers, they will be able to:

- Select the appropriate and most effective mobile social media site for its program
- Identify which paid advertisement will drive the most traffic
- Design effective mobile apps for effective marketing for niche application like LBS, gaming, etc.

For example, by analyzing consumer mobile behavior, major advertisers found that customers send SMSs more efficiently and quickly with mobile apps like "Whatsapp." The Apps are able to attract paid advertisements and gain popularity. As a marketer, this information provides an indication that the Apps will give a new marketing channel for products and services that text messaging customers may be interested in based on what they do with mobile services.

Monitoring data is, therefore, valuable to a company in order to improve an MSM marketing strategy so the information tracked and analyzed is then applied to improve the strategy.

The process typically involves looking at thousands (or even millions) of conversations and can take up a lot of time. If you are wise, you will put automated monitoring systems in place to do it for you.

You will have to decide what you need to track and analyze and how much you want to invest in analyses. There are plenty of tools from free software like Google Alerts, BlogPulse, or Radian 6, an automated trend discovery system for mobile and social networks that analyzes and reports on daily activity.

Common priority metrics you should measure in a social media campaign include:

- Interaction using social networks and mobile apps
- Sales conversion
- Leads generation
- Profits
- Search marketing
- Brand metrics
- PR
- Customer interaction and retention

Data sought includes:

- Number of transactions
- Number of new-to-file customers
- Changes in repeat customers
- Number of customer referrals
- Uplift in other marketing channels

Digital marketers and PR professionals have a variety of entry-level free tools and enterprise platforms available to do the necessary monitoring. You just have to decide and customize your plan of action for your Brand.

The final test and the true measurement of your success is the number of conversions, or any activity that can be directly or indirectly monetized.

CHAPTER 12

Planning for your International Penetration—MSM usage in Asia Pacific countries

With economic analysts forecasting China to become the growth engine for global economic growth for the next twenty years for mobile related technologies, many Western corporations are planning to realign their global strategies to gain a presence in China and other Asian markets.

Usage of mobile social media in Countries like China is increasing and reaching a wider audience than ever. However, no individual mobile or social networking services is able to dominate mobile social media in the world; sometimes, we see them available only in specific countries.

This is because some governments place restrictions on the internet (in countries such as Myanmar and China) and also due to cultural differences and language barriers. New mobile social media sites are developing in every country, with new SNSs being introduced in different language platforms and around the world.

Comscore reported that Facebook is the leading SNS among the different markets in Asia Pacific, Japan, South Korea, Taiwan, Indonesia, India, and China.

Consumers in the Asia-Pacific region have become more aware of mobile and social networking platform. They have become more highly influenced by online advertising. Consumers' opinions posted online are usually preferred and will be accepted with more confidence as confidence in using MSMs increases. Users tend to value opinions posted by friends and will always check on reviews or comments as a source of information.

The Asia-Pacific MSM market is very diverse and progressing very rapidly. Typically, due to cultural differences, the mobile and social networking services have evolved differently from those of North America and Europe.

Niche social media behavior in these regions is prone to building mobile social media around the trait of the current lifestyle, local language, and the exposure to the digital age. The majority of netizens are made up of young people and they have more digital self-expression.

Such self-expression has driven consumer interest in online games, and even on Bulletin Board System (BBS) forums, where users have the tendency to stay anonymous but to use virtual expression via avatars in communication with friends. Such avatars are usually their iconic heroes of the online games.

This format and concept is noticed in most of the mobile and social networking sites in Taiwan, South Korea, Thailand, Vietnam, and China.

Developed Asian markets have jumped on the bandwagon with the use of mobile social networking, which has been further extended through the massive usage of smartphones, mobile social sites, and mobile extension portals to powerhouse internet social networking sites.

According to a report from CASBA—China, 65% of the total online population in the Asia-Pacific region visited a social networking site in June 2011, reaching a total of 350.3 million visitors, including China. Facebook.com ranked as the top social network across the majority of different countries in the Asia pacific region, while competing Social networking sites did better in certain markets, including:

- RenRen and Weibo in China
- Orkut in India, Mixi.jp in Japan, CyWorld in South Korea, and Wretch.cc in Taiwan

Among the leading SNSs, most of them are based in their local language, and this signifies the Asia pacific region differentiation in the mobile social media marketcompared to US, European and other regions.

As of February 2010, analysts reported that the total internet audience aged 15 and underat home and work locations for Social Networking reach will reach 50.8%. This figure excludes user visits from public computers such as internet cafes or access from mobile phones.

This reach is further boosted with global mobile connections. In the Asia-Pacific region, according to the GSMA Asia-Pacific Mobile Observatory 2011 report, mobile penetration will reach a landmark three billion connections in the first quarter of 2012. By 2015, it is expected that the region will reach 4.1 billion connections, growing at twice the rate of Europe and North America, and will account for 40 per cent of mobile data traffic worldwide.

This trend will grow tremendously, as almost 35% of the mobile users, especially in Thailand, India, Laos, Cambodia, Vietnam, Indonesia and China, usually surf the internet via their lower-end phones. The higher-end phones like Android, Apple, Sony, or Blackberry are only used among the high-income class.

This will cause extensive growth in penetration of mobile services in Asia Pacific as mobile operators in the region's major markets will increase their investment in distribution of mobile connections to wider rural areas. This will increase their revenues and spending on capital expenditure, significantly more than their counterparts in other parts of the world.

Other key areas of improvements include:

-   Introduction of low-cost Smart-type handphone and reduction in charge for mobile phone usage
-   Mobile internet-enabled devices will take up a secondary portion of the cell phone markets and the adaptabilities of carrier to cope with wider applications.

- Introducing new innovative business model to bring down cost through better distribution strategies like location based service and expansion of network coverage to rural areas would make use of these services economically viable for consumers.

With such gains in investments and popularity in the mobile arena, social networking is thus gaining mobility. As online social networking providers add mobile interfaces to their services, numerous specialized mobile-centric social networks are expected to emerge.

Regional differences

Social media is huge in Asia, but very distinct from the Western world in several aspects. Therefore, marketers will need to understand that the regional differences among the social customers are significant. When determining how to reach the social customer in each global region, they will need to consider various factors, including:

1) **Trends of mobile technology and communication**
   The prevalence of tablet technology and applications, and their integration with the advancement in geolocation technologies should be considered.

2) **Adoption**
   It is necessary understand the impact of how social customers can adapt to new technological changes in mobile and social communication through mobile social media.

3) **Language and Culture**

Learn the language. It may not be necessary to be fluent, but you should be able to grasp the minimal language requirement that could be applied to the daily interaction on your platform. Understand the cultural difference in your local market to the global arena to be able to find a common understanding between users so that international users can also use your services.

4) **Rules and regulations**

Analyze how the local economic factors affect your branding effort in your new market, as sufficient funding is necessary to ensure your marketing budget will cover areas like privacy, fair exposure, transparency, intellectual property, censorship, net neutrality, and government and corporate control for all emerging technologies.

5) **Competition**

Look for a niche or competitive edge. This is to ensure that your branding efforts will succeed against the competitors'. Find out how your local social customer will react to your products and services.

Practical Mobile and Social Media Marketing in China

During the course of my internship in China under an event organization company in Hong Kong, I was attached to a Beijing office and working on several projects in the event organization at the China International Exhibition Center. This involvedintensive co-ordination with major clients in

Japan, the UK, Germany, and other European countries. My responsibilities included to support all facets of planning events, social marketing, advertisement planning, seminars, and online advertisements, which includedthe introduction of their show event to major manufacturing industries throughout China via social media marketing.

My 20-month internship was a daunting experience that coincided with new developments of the mobile technology, the launch of the E-ink reader and Androd V2.1 color tablet reader. The tablet has been doing well in the China social media landscape, when major SNSs like Youku and RenRen has just listed their IPOs on the Nasdaq.

In the Next Chapter, I will walk you through the landscape of China's Mobile Social Media environment as well as their netizens' trend on consumption of information and the various Mobile social media platforms that marketers need to approach, with a practical, local-oriented way of engagement with the Chinese audience.

Guanxi—Chinese Social Networking

Before venturing any social media marketing endeavors in China, the marketers should appreciate the concept of "Guanxi."

Guanxi means relationships and connections. In the Chinese business world, however, it is also understood as the network of relationships among various individuals that connect and cooperate together with goodwill and obligation, with emphasis on shared experience. This Word is rooted very deeply in the social-cultural society in China, and has been for millennia.

It boils down to exchanging favors, which are expected to be done regularly and voluntarily. Therefore, it is an important concept to understand if your business is to function effectively in Chinese society.

Mobile social networks have, therefore, become closely tied in with Guanxi networks. Therefore, in China, with consideration of most users appreciating their cultural reliability of Guanxi, messages that were sent or spread via mobile communication and social networking always enjoys high credibility, while mutual obligation and respect contributes to the acceptance of the messaging within the mobile social networks.

The Demographics of Chinese Mobile Internet Users

Status quo of social media in China: According to the latest report released by CNNIC, the Internet Society of China, in June 2012, China has 538 million netizens, including 128 million Bulletin Board user; and almost 960 million mobile phone users, with almost 388 million mobile internet users and almost 308 million are social network services user using multiple platforms in China itself.

Almost 66.8% of these users are young people below 25, with students making up more than one in three of all social users. The older demographic group has over 48% of internet users, ranging from 30 to 59 years old.

The majority of the users are students and lower income users, where cost is the main concern;the mobile internet users are believed to have breached 380 million in the first quarter of 2012.

The following is an overview of the younger demographic:

- 65% of online users' primary purpose of mobile social networking is simply keeping in touch with friends and colleagues
- The main purposes of 48% include browsing information, killing time, playing games, and making new friends.
- About 20% will look at business pages or branding advertisements.
- About 60% will do online purchases for electronic products such as mobile phones, cameras, DIY hardware, computer peripherals, and other accessories.

Social shopping and marketing have been recently boosted by cross-promotions and cooperation between different mobile, social networking platforms and online shopping portals. Jiepang, the leading mobile social networking site cross-promoted some of its main advertisers, with advertisements also showing up in Weibo and RenRen.

Regarding mobile markets, a recent CNNIC survey revealed that frequent social media users in China are big users. They access social media on mobile phones. It is sometimes easier for lower income individuals to buy the mobile phone than the computers, as these are blue collar users who prefer instant communication with the handheld mobile phones.

Text messaging is the most common means of communication with cell phones, which are mostly WAP enabled. With 3G mobile coming onto the scene, smartphone handsets have also found their way into the Chinese market. Accordingly, users have also leaped into apps markets, as seen in other regions.

Chinese users are busy chatting, texting, and playing with apps and games on mobiles as intensively as you'll find in other global cities. The new generations of devices have opened up another new landscape for mobile internet users, and around two thirds (70%) of users are already accessing mobile web content. This is causing a fast take up of cheaper mobile internet-enabled devices because everyone prefers a smartphone.

Given this trend, it is clear the SNSswill continue to develop mobile friendly sites and users will be more prone to networking through their mobile devices.

Chinese Social Media Channels

Taking a closer look at the most visited sites in China, we noticed that web portals like SinaWeibo, Kaixin and RenRen rank among the top favourite sites. Dominating the local Internet market, Chinese portals offer a wide array of social media services, including:

- Video sharing
- Micro-blog, blogging
- Wikis
- eCommerce
- Online trade

- Bulletin Board and forums
- Location-based services
- Instant messaging
- Photo sharing
- Social gaming
- Social bookmarking services

The social media channels are some of the more popular examples of popular platforms, and these landscapes are frequently changing, as there are always more types of mobile and social network sites in China becoming available.

When working with Chinese social media, marketers should take note that the Mobile and Social Networking sites in China are not the same as their western counterparts, like Twitter or Facebook. The function of the sites may be similar;however, they use different approaches and have different targeted consumers. Therefore, advertising campaigns that work on Facebook may not work on RenRen.

The demographics, languages, audiences, behaviors, and cultures are totally different from one another. Marketers need to understand that a Western approach or strategy needs to be revised and fine-tuned. This requiresdue consideration of the differences in social economics and users' interests, preferences, cultural respect, and etiquette.

With strong market growth and a country with top tier modern cities, it is no surprise that many global internet and branding companies rushed to China without much hesitation in the early 2000s. Internet giants such as Yahoo, Google, Amazon, AOL, and EBay met with failure, and has almost all withdrawn from the massive market, or been secluded to a corner in China's internet landscape, awaiting new opportunities.

Their failure was most probably from the lack of research into local culture, implementation, and adaptation to the local market. Although some of these Internet giants' ventures did not progress well, this has not stopped the growing interest in the Chinese internet industry.

Driven by an investors' interest in Chinese internet companies, many Chinese companies took investors' advice and have managed to go public on the NASDAQ with their IPOs. Companies like Youku, DangDang, and RenRen managed to gain investors' interest with large investments, and some upcoming IPOs in 2012 include: Taobao, VANCL, TUDOU, Taomee, Qunar, LaShou, Meituan, all of which provide services on the internet.

These listings will provide the new Chinese giant internet companies the resources to develop new innovative technologies.

Parallel Mobile Social Media Practice with a Difference

Chinese netizens like and opt for varieties of services like gaming portals, entertainment sites, social networks, and many others. With all this happening in the country (with the largest population in the world), the Chinese Government has always been careful and implemented censorship to ensure the internet will not cause and outflow of information, while carefully balancing this with the commercial point of view.

They try to protect their local companies' interest to ensure that their internet companies will be able to face local competition among themselves. This is opposed to having to face the major western social platforms, which may easily influence their local netizens, or at least provide them breathing space to catch up with the Western big boys like Facebook and Twitter. China has the rights to implement its rules. Thus, foreign companies who visits China will need to respect their rules and subject their companies to China's strict government censorships.

Differences in Western and Chinese Business Models

In China, users of mobile and social networks may need to pay a membership fee for certain sites, which, consequently, have become highly profitable. Many netizens are attracted to these sites for virtual games, with rewards of virtual currencies, which generate up to five billion US dollars per year in revenues for their developers, since marketers are motivated to put up fan pages for their brands for maximum effectiveness.

This opens up huge potentials for major brands—for example, Volkswagen with Kaixin and Burberry with Jiepang. Recent successful branding campaigns created enormous buzz through viral influence by peers using location-based services. A top fashion brand, LV, integrated with Youku and Jiepang, offering branded "virtual badges" for users who "checked-in" at boutiques, and putting users in the running to win tickets to store launches and other events. The company cross promotes using a Youku Video of the product on Jiepang and manage to attract young buyers, who are out to collect Jiepang's Virtual badges on their

SNS's profile with the Brand Logo. This resulted in a successful buzz about the brand and good sales at the same time.

From the campaign analyst perspective, it has been established that peer-to-peer referral is very effective in China. By engaging with key bloggers and social networking sites, a large number of followers can be reached. These findings reveal that Chinese society is avidly using social networking channels to engage with friends, share ideas, and discuss brands. Peer pressure to maintain status is particularly potent in China.

How Social Media Work in China

BBS Forum—In 1994, China's Bulletin Board system (BBS), which is comprised of blogs and forums, was launched. The system was a trendsetter then, and distinguished itself from the web in other global markets. BBS represents a favorite destination for netizens and provides a higher level of commitment, as users found it a good site for sharing images and videos at that period of time. This system is used more for B2C users and the general consumers. The most famous message board in China is Tianya. However, in recent years, its popularity has been overtaken by social networking sites like Qzone, 51.com, Xiaonei, Kaixin001, and others.

Blogging—Chinese people like sharing their ideas online—creating poems, gossip and writing reviews—but they usually are written Chinese. Generally, blogs in China are mostly industry based and are used by companies, celebrities, or organizations. Blogging will also benefit from the functions of micro blogging such as social bookmarking or mobile phone texting. Widely used blog hosting platforms include Sina, Sohu and Weibo

Micro-blogs—Similar to Twitter, microblogs are websites that allow netizens to post short (140-160 characters) posts. Chinese microbloggers prefer to send short gossip messages, but traders and advertisers have exploited the service to include promotions and product links. The leading microblog host in China is SinaWeibo.

Instant Messaging—Instant messaging (IM) is used by almost 95% of internet users with Microsoft Windows Live Messenger (MSN) accounts. The Chinese counterpart to MSN is powered by QQ. QQ live chat is popular, and it's main platform provider has a user base of up to 650 Million people.

Social Networks Systems—SMS plays an increasingly important role in mobile social media in China. Although most users choose a social network according to the number of their known friends, colleagues, or classmates who are members, the main purpose for joining such networks is entertainment and gaming. Among the top social networking sites, Tencent (QQ) and Qzone are the biggest.

Similar to the global arena, there are also niche business-related sites that are focused to professional networking and recruiting use, as with the LinkedIn format (e.g., Ushi.cn) and location-based service platform sites like Jiepang, which has some similarities in function with Foursquare.

Video—Watching videos is one of the favorite pastimes of Chinese Internet users. Local websites like Tudou and Youku are teaming with Chinese broadcasters to provide integrated TV networks;the main reason for this integration is that the Chinese like to watch soap opera and drama shows online. A large number of movies and some user generated or self-created media productsare also upload to these video sites. Internet TV websites are another source for videos, and the three most popular sitesare Uitv, UUsee, and v.china.com.

Location-Based Services

The location based marketing platform provides entertainment services and check-in with similarities with Foursquare;this has been effective also in video advertisements. This can be effective for rural and city areas, as it is best suited for B2C companies and especially for viewers to locate their branch shops in rural areas as well as in the main cities. Jiepang's platform provides users with information or entertainment services through a mobile device and networks that have the ability to identify the geographical location of the device.

Photo Sharing—With Chinesemobile platforms booming, and almost every new model of phone comes with a built-in camera, netizens are able to upload and share their photos on the mobile social media, with many popular sites like Yupoo, Roco, Bababian. The site provides a one-stop shop for photo-related services, like editing, sharing, searching, and slide show clips.

Online Trade—The three main sites are Taobao, Paipai, and 360 Buy. They are similar to auction sites and function quite similarly to eBay, especially in the case of Paipai. China has another famous portal called Alibaba. It is a trade directory site where most of the manufacturers in China are listed. Alibaba offers easy means for traders to communicate with each other, where advertiser can showcase their products, and it comes with a chatline, newsletter, and email for easy communication between manufacturers with traders all around the word.

Social bookmarking—Social bookmarking is popular, especially when it works similarly to microblogging in China. The general operation concept is similar to Digg or Twitter in terms of functionality. However, here, web users like to view popular topics and gossip on celebrities, deals of the day, or political related articles. Many people prefer this channel to search for information rather than using search engines. As Chinese netizens'are deeply concerned with Guanxi (described earlier in the present chapter)they will rely on their fellow netizens to share information. For this major difference, social bookmarking sites are very much preferred and are capable to generate high-volume traffic and effective for marketing. Popular social bookmarking websites include Baidu, Soucang, QQ shuqian, JiaThis, bShare. cn, Passit, Baidu Bookmarks, and Feixin (China Mobile).

While tablet technology expands and evolves, it will be an integral tool for netizens in the years to come, and Android operating system used for both tablet and smartphone is widely used due to its open programming system.

Since its introduction, many tablet manufacturers in China are able to produce low price tablets with color screens because of the open-source Android operating system. Tablet applications with functions like geolocation, gaming, GPS, eBook reading, chatline, social bookmarking, text messaging with Chinese language have also become entrenched as supporting sub-tools in the MSM landscape in China.

Both smartphone and tablet apps have a place in the mobile social media channels in China. There are some specific online platforms in China that would deserve further study, including online gaming, wikis (such as Hudong), search marketing with Baidu, photo sharing, and online music.

The Chinese Language Barrier: "How Can you See the Rainbow if you Don't Go out in the Rain?"

The Chinese language is notoriously difficult for many Westerners, as it is very different from English.

The most obvious difference is that Chinese words are not constructed with alphabets, and character construction are made out of strokes written according to a few set of rules; and besides, Chinese and English grammar are radically different. China has been held together by a common written system and a common Han Yu language, which is in mandarin dialect (or "Pu Tong Hua"), so that people from all over China can communicate through writing.

Therefore, in order for one to learn Chinese, it will take a person months to pick up the language while understanding its culture and history. Luckily, with some Google translation or dictionary at hand, it may not seem as daunting. Nevertheless, the truth is that most online translation tools are only 30% accurate at getting it right, and even interpreters sometime may not be able to translate from Chinese to English accurately.

However, this restriction has been slightly overcome by a new phenomenon, where netizens are starting to use a communized chatline internet language. This is similar to SMS, except the base reference is from Chinese words, and those who practice need to be able to at least to converse in Chinese to understand the abbreviation. This language is known as "Chinese Internet language": Wangluo Yu Yan.

A simple format will be Slang words like 牛 (niu), which symbolizes "fierce" or "strong" (originally meaning "ox" or "cow"). "88" (baba) is short for "bye bye".

Wangluo Yu Yan is commonplace in online chats, blogs, microblogs, and more. One of the characteristics of such internet terms is that they could spread easily by the younger generation since millions of bloggers are using it. It is now very much being used as text message language also between Chinese people living in different cities.

Digital friends or Real life friends—culture etiquette.
Due to the strict cultural and Confucian values practiced by the Chinese, netizens, especially between the ages of 14-22, feel the need to channel themselves towards the internet. This enables them to express themselves in a more liberating manner, to their friends online, especially on Qzone, as the SNS is usually used by students, while more mature user are usually found on RenRen or Kaixin.

The average netizens express themselves from behind digital avatars, which are constructed at the SNS as a representation of the netizens with their profile. These avatars are an important part of many netizens' online identity, whether their identity is real to life or not.

For Western social media users, friends on the social networking sites usually represent themselves as actual real-life people;however, in China, the tendency to add digital avatars that are strangers as friends is more common. This symbolizes a better way of expression in China, and usually the avatars are all quite able to express themselves and comment on the SNS. With this prevalence of avatars, SNS allows further expression and customization. This is manifested by incorporating games, rewards, and community interaction that bring entertainment values that are appealing to the users, who find it fun and, at the same time, liberating. Due to the long times spent in commuting, Chinese users are constantly looking for entertainment and some form of "escape" and to add less stressful elements into their daily lives.

Due to the strong value of sharing and actively participating within the BBS culture, the Chinese netizens have been migrating from BBS to social networking sites with much anticipation of similar functions. Thus, for marketers to penetrate to the arena in China, they should understand the different functionality of SNS available and spend some time in the BBS forum to familiarize themselves with this platform as it has been effective in gathering and creating buzz with the viral marketing for branding purposes.

While not giving the BBS culture a miss, marketers will be able to adapt to mobile social networking sites with more efficiency, as many Chinese net users rely on both mobile and social networking sites as a primary source of easy accessible entertainment. The Bulletin Board system (BBS) is still very popular in China, and these will undoubtedly be upgraded in functionality, and areunlikely to disappear in the near future.

Given the above, marketers will need to take into account these difference between Western and Chinese Internet users and to adopt them if they want their marketing efforts to be effective.

CHAPTER 13

Harnessing the power of cloud for Mobile social media

With already 70% of users in China accessing the internet via mobile internet enabled device; the social wave has hit strongly with analyst believing that the demographic of mobile users will far exceed any other technology in the World. Marketers therefore will need to prepare and incorporate the mobile aspect as part of the mobile social media venture.

As technology advances, the adoption of mobile devices grow, businesses will need to fundamentally change their operations to take advantage of the new capabilities.

The shifts in consumer behavior as a result of mobile social media and the cloud are profound. The cloud is providing data storage for consumer and enterprise data, scaling capacity for small companies to develop new services and new application content distribution models.

These new breeds of devices will have Internet connectivity to the "cloud" where it can be accessed wherever you go via today's powerful 4G networks or Wi-Fi which provides the power of real time visibility.

Thanks to cloud computing, all netizens can now use your mobile devices to surf the Web, check email, update your status on social media networks or shop online.

While digital photos have revolutionized photography, they also take up a lot of hard drive space and this means storage and retrieval may be a problem for many users. Google has since developed a free photo management and editing software called Picasa. One of its coolest features is Picasa Web Albums, which syncs and shares photo albums of your choice to the Web. This means that you can park many pictures on Picasa Cloud storage system and using your mobile phone, you can access to the pictures anytime.

The Amazon MP3™ Music application is one good example which overcomes storage limitations by introducing the Amazon Cloud player, a service that will upload 5GB of your music and playlists for free. It enables any of your mobile internet enabled devices that are signed into your Amazon MP3 account to stream their favourites from a complete library of songs at their fingertips over 3G, 4G or Wi-Fi, without using up any local storage from their handheld device.

With such cloud based services, users can access movies, music, data via smartphones or your mobile tablets which you can have the same content on both devices. Such services change the way we edit documents, manage files, read books and more.

The cloud has completely altered a major sector in offline computing. In the past, if your laptop crashed, you were at risk of losing everything. Now users are able to control their entire digital world (in the cloud)—from organizing family photos to updating my work documents—without having to back up all of their media from their personal hardware.

Cloud computing simplifies the entire process. If your laptop does crash, data stored in the cloud will still be there for you to retrieve it, by just accessing to your personal account hosted in the cloud.

Cloud computing involves using the internet to provide the resources and services for computing such as mobile devices, web browsers, net and other formats. The platform involves the architecture of the hardware and software structures that include the computer's operating system, programming languages, GUI, and other components.

There are several components that make up the architecture of cloud computing. These components include clients, services, platforms, applications, storage, and infrastructure some of the attributes are as follows:

- The service is provided by the cloud provider hosting Company
- The service is always available
- The interface to a service is defined
- The provider of the service will maintain, enhance, and resolve any problems with the service
- Any service can be allocated a cost

Cloud services can range from low level services that require an API, like storage or database access, or a high level service like an application.

Cloud computing also may prove to be an ideal strategy for reaping the full benefit of mobile devices by allowing companies to essentially push their application services out to employees or registered users to access the company database in the cloud.

Sample Architecture of Cloud controller

Within the cloud model, there are usually three different service layers, namely:

1. Infrastructure as a Service (IaaS)
2. Platform as a Service (PaaS)
3. Software as a Service (SaaS)

These three layers support each other and the relationships between the layers remain relatively stable.

In addition, there is also the hardware layer which is owned and operated by the cloud service provider.

The Hardware Layer

The hardware layer refers to the physical hardware that provides actual resources which makes up the cloud. Often, hardware resources are inexpensive and are not fault tolerant. Redundancy is achieved simply by utilizing multiple hardware platforms while fault tolerance is provided at other layers so that any hardware failure will not noticed by the users.

Infrastructure as a Service (IaaS)

It provides grids cluster or virtualization layer networks, storage and systems software designed to provide basic computer networking, load balancing, content delivery networks, routing, commodity data storage, and virtualized operating system hosting.

Instead of purchasing servers or even hosted services, IaaS customers can create and remove virtual machines and network them together at will. This hardware virtualization enables companies to optimize the use of physical computer resources. This reduces the need to buy and operate physical servers, data storage systems, or networking resources. For this IaaS processes, you can outsource your hardware needs to someone else.

Some of the biggest names using IaaS include Amazon and Microsoft.

Platform as a Service (PaaS)

The platform layer works in virtualized hardware environments with virtual machines and provides a platform in which software applications are developed. This is usually web based. It is an immediate abstraction of the underlying infrastructure.

At this layer, customers do not manage their virtual machines; they merely create applications within an existing Application programming interface (API) or programming language. The processing power of these virtual machine and storage power can be dynamically changed based on actual business requirement on demand as they occur. Clients merely create their own programs which are hosted by the platform services they are paying for which include; Web application management, application design, app hosting, storage, security, and app development.

Software as a Service (SaaS)
It provides network-based access to commercially available software like Gmail, Google Docs, Quickbooks and etc.

SaaS represents the potential for a lower-cost method for businesses to use software. For users whom need to interact frequently with their software, it is made accessible through a web browser.

Such applications can be email, customer relationship management, and other office productivity applications. Enterprise services can be billed monthly or by usage, while software as service offered directly to consumers, such as email, is often provided for free.

For mobile and social networking users, the use of applications that is available via cloud computing is probably the most important aspect of the cloud computing technology. Both Mobile and Web applications are the components that most end users utilize with the cloud computing.

These applications vary from popular social networking sites such as, Foursquare, Jiepang, MySpace, Facebook, Twitter and LinkedIn to other sites; such as YouTube, Youku and Blogger. Such Mobile and Social Networking sites utilize cloud computing technology and architecture to provide a variety of applications and resources to customers with easy access from a variety of computing platforms.

With the mass usage of Wi-fi and availability of wireless networks, it has helped in the proliferation of cloud computing and the Mobile social networking applications. The use of smart phones to access online applications, for texting, Music streaming, Videos and gaming have grown tremendously. This is another aspect of cloud computing that has benefited from the technology.

Cloud computing will further change the way businesses use the internet to interact with customers.

Businesses will save on infrastructure cost and remote Call centers or off-shore accounting base and other business departments will utilize cloud computing as a method of providing data, services, and information to their clients, responding to customer inquiries and customer relationship management (CRM) tools are being used for more effective monitoring using cloud computing technology.

Web 3.0 with cloud computing is evolving so fast that major businesses or specialized marketers that do not embrace the technology might be left behind very quickly. This is due to the fact that, in the very near future, there will be a new internet landscape in the horizonthat there will change how businesses are being conducted.

Mobile technology in particular, is going to move up another level which will have a significant impact on the way we live and the way we conduct business today.

When you are equipped with the information provided in this book; start thinking about how to implement the different developments in the mobile and social networking landscapesthat may serve to improve your business. Ask yourself the following questions:

- Do we need to start building new mobile friendly site for our company featuring our products and services?
- Will using mobile technology like Mcommerce enables customers to purchase and pay for our products or services via their mobile phones?
- Do we need to retrain our staffs to be able to capitalize on the use of mobile social media technology?
- Does using mobile social media networking to interact with our customers and potential ensure your business is providing the products and services that they need?
- Do you need to engage location-based technologies to enable you to more effectively target potential customers?
- Do we need to introduce GPS Mobile gadgets to our field operation staff so that they are exposed to Geo-location technology?
- Do you expect to get immediate response to special offers by sending SMS to customer via their mobile phones?
- Maybe we should set up a team to organize our business operation to incorporate with Mobile social media technology
- Do we need to consider to provide operation staff with smartphones in order to be more efficient and more productive in their work roles?
- Will mobile social media save us travelling trips but yet still increase the number of sales contacts and sales made?

207

- Will QR code mobile technologies help our business operation in its enterprising process?
- Will incorporating QR code technology in your website or mobisite make your marketing more effective and engaging with customers?
- Is video technology able to attract and communicate with more customers more effectively?
- Can mobile social media marketing help to increase conversion of sales withina landing page?
- Can the use of virtual trade shows with videos help you increase the number of viable leads?
- Can product coding or venue coding with QR coding technology increase lead generation at trade show events or help to generate more visits to your booths or shops?
- Can cloud-computing technology help your office provides more streaming service for your clients?
- Can incorporating cloud computing to your business help you to save on infrastructure and hardware purchase costs?

Vision of the future

Imagine 10 years from now, a post 90's youngster would probably have a day like this: On her way to work, a car accident occurred and she is caught in a traffic jam. Using a social GPS system, she notices other drivers heading to the same direction and they are taking another route with less traffic. She follows them as well and successfully avoids a traffic jam. As she passes a supermarket, a reminder on her mobile phone suggests that there is no milk left at home.

To choose the brand of milk to buy, she scans the bar code on the new brand of milk and she instantly gets its sales statistics and online reviews. Later, at a bookstore, a new book by her favourite author catches her attention. As she takes a copy and flips the pages, her mobile phone browser automatically loads the book's page on Douban (a Chinese Web 2.0 website) providing reviews and recommendations for movies, books and music. It shows the ratings and list of reviews by other users, as well. Through these reviews, she finds anebook dealer on Taobao—China's largest Internet retail platform that offers goods at the lowest prices. She then decides to order the ebook and noted in her memo, a reminder to order the book from Taobao, when she is back home or at anytime when she is free to download the book.

At night, she meets up with some friends for supper at a new restaurant, but she has difficulty finding the place. So, she selects the social mapping site on her mobile phone to identify where both her friend's and her own location on the map. Her mobile GPS system on her phone immediate gives the correct co-ordinates and she found the location just in time to meet her friends. At dinner, she took pictures with her friends and their location is automatically labelled on it together with the time and the names of her friends. The dinner ends early, so she decides to visit a local bar.

It is crowded when she arrives, as it is the weekend. She opens up the Hook-Me-Up application on her phone to look for someone to chat with. It searches for other nearby devices with this feature turned on. By checking the compatibility of different users' profiles on Douban, it returns a list with three young men on it.

After several rounds of text messages, she was approached by one of them and they start a great conversation for the night.

Social computing will enter our lives faster than we think. It will soon become a single, cohesive experience embedded in our daily activities and technologies. As mobile platforms take center stage, we could foresee its application scope to quickly expand beyond Web 2.0 to become an indispensable component of users' offline experiences. Emerging mobile social computing applications will introduce new dimensions to the meaning of "social networking" by taking us into a new era of connected experiences unbounded by distance, time, location or any physical constraints.

GLOSSARY

Mobile Social Media Glossary

The A to Z glossary of common social media terms

AdSense: Google's pay-per-click, context-relevant program available to blog and web publishers as a way to create revenue. A small, text-based ad that can be incorporated and displayed as part of website or blog's content. The site owner receives a fee each time a web surfer clicks on the advertiser's ad.

Advertiser: The person selling the goods, media or service; also known as the Merchant. This person affiliates by sending traffic to it's website after a product or service is purchased.

Affiliate marketing: Using one website to drive traffic to another is a form of online marketing.

Adwords: the advertiser program that populates the Adsense program. The advertiser pay Google on a per click basis.

Aggregator: A web-based tool or desktop application that collects syndicated content and bring them together in one place.

Akismet: A comment spam filter popular with WordPress blog.

Alerts: A tool to get a search engine to tell you whenever a new page is published on the web, which includes your specific keyword.

App: An application that performs a specific function on your computer or handheld device.

Admob: It is an advertising platform which serves mobile banner and text ads across mobile websites and handset applications.

Authenticity: the practice of being authentic, real, genuine, committed in online interactions

Avatar: A graphical image or likeness that replaces a photo of the author of the content on a blog. This may not be an authentic representation of the person behind the image.

Autoresponder: A program that sends an automatic form response to incoming emails.

Banner: A graphical display ad that can be displayed on a website or blog. Banners are typically created in a variety of standard sizes.

Blog Hosting Service: An online-based service that hosts online blogs and that provides bloggers with the online tools and template which are needed to create, publish, and manage their blog.

Blogger: The writer or creator of a blog.

Blogging: The act of writing and publishing a blog.

Badge: An image, normally displayed on a blog, which signifies the blogger's participation in an event, contest, or social movement.

Blogroll: A list of recommended related friendly blogs.

Bookmarking: save the address of a website or item of content, either in your browser, or on a social bookmarking site like Diigo and Delicious.

Bookmarklet: A widget bookmark containing scripting code, usually written in JavaScript that allows the user to perform a function.

Bulletin Boards: A digital online collaboration for sharing and chating, where users connected with a central server to post and read parametric messages. The concept is similar to a forum except the template format is less congested.

Conversion Rate: Percentage of clicks of people who actually clickon it and respond to an ad displayed on a blog or webpage, compared to the number of people who just see the ad, but never click on it

Content: The combination of text, graphics, photographs, animations, audio, video, and other multimedia elements used to populate and create a blog, vlog, or website.

Campaign: An online campaign is a planned coordinated marketing program, delivered at intervals, with the goal of conducting a sales promotion exercise or increasing the sales of a product.

Chat online: Interaction on a web site, with a number of people adding text items one after the other into the same space at the same.

Cloud computing: Refers to the application or service hosted on the cloud and can be accessed by users from anywhere rather than being tied to a particular machine.

Cloud: It serves as a hosting infrastructure for mobile and social media application, services and network. The cloud can host online application, user information and storage of data where user can access anytime.

Content Management System: (CMS): Central menu software that allows user to add to, edit and update content on your site with no HTML knowledge, they offer the ability to create static web pages, document stores, blog, wikis, and other tools.

Conversation: Being engaged, get into conversation through blogging, commenting or contributing to forums, which is the currency of social networking.

Earnings Per click (EPC): Average earnings per 100 clicks. A relative rating that describes the ability to turn clicks into commissions.

Creative Commons: An alternative licensing system that offers creators the ability to fine-tune their copyright, facilitating the ways in which others may use their works with a Creative commons license.

Dashboard: the administration area on your website or blog which allows you to post, check traffic, upload files, manage comments, widget and your template setting and layout. It is the major control centre where user can also access to email, statistic etc.

Earnings Per click (EPC): Average earnings per 100 clicks. A relative rating that describes the ability to turn clicks into commissions.

Ecommerce Website: A website design to sell products online that will be shipped to the customer once payment is received. This type of website has a shopping cart feature that allows customer (web surfers) to safely and securely place their orders using a major credit card or another online payment method.

Favorite: a Bookmarking process of content or updates in social networks for sharing.

Feature Phone: Refers to the low end mobile phone that has less computing ability than a smartphone.

Forums: Forums are useful where you want an open discussion on subject and various topics on websites. It allows people to post messages or comment on existing messages asynchronously.

Geotagging: the process of adding location-based metadata to media such as picture, graphics, video or online maps, Geotagging integrates with location services provider for services based on location.

Geolocation is the identification of a physical venue based on geographic location of an object, such as a mobile phone, or a mobile internet enabled device. Geolocation may refer to the practice of assessing the location.

Gadget: Also known as Gidzmo, is a technological product such as smart device or an electronic unit that has a particular function.

Hit: A single hit is equivalent to one visitor to a website or blog, or one person viewing a specific webpage. It can be used for web analytics.

HTML: (Hypertext Markup Language): A popular programming language used to create webpages, online documents, blogs and websites. HTML defines the structure and layout of a blog or webpage and allows for the use of hyperlinks.

Influencer: A person specialized in a specific subject and is highly recognized in an online community with the ability to convince others

Instant Messaging (IM): Chat with another person, using an IM tool like MSN instant messenger, Yahoo Messenger or Google Talk.

Listening: This refers to the art of skimming feed to see what topic are buzzing up, and also setting up searches that monitor certain news, brand name or the name of your organization when it is mentioned in the internet.

Merchant Account: Offered by a merchant account provider, such as a bank or financial institution, this is what's required for a business operator to be able to accept credit card payments. The merchant will be charged various fees to be able to accept credit card payments for the sale of goods and services over the internet.

Mobile Blogging: The ability to create and publish blog content using a wireless PDA, smart phone, or a mobile enabled device that's connected to the wireless web.

Mobile browser: An Internet browser which runs on a mobile phone.

Metadata: Information such as titles, descriptions, tags and captions that describes a media item such as a video, link, photo or blog post.

Micro-blogging: A short messages broadcasting tool for sending 140 character messages to other subscribers of web services. Its content is typically smaller and allows users to exchange small elements of content such as short sentences, individual images, or video links.

Moblogging: Short form for mobile blogging or meaning posting to your blog via your mobile phone.

Monetization: Website monetization is the process of converting existing traffic being sent to a particular website into revenue, the approach to making money from your online platform usually by display advertising, subscription, affiliate links, or context advertising.

Measurement: Metrics applied in mobile and social networking services is an emerging discipline. It is used for tracking the social media use with combination of web-stats package, calls to action, surveys, subscriptionsand downloads.

Mobile Application (APP): This is a software that runs on mobile internet enabled device that will allow the device to perform specific tasks.

Multimedia Content: Content that uses a combination of different content forms. Multimedia includes a combination of text, images, animation, video, sound or other digital media forms.

MyBlogLog: A yahoo-owned community and social networking site that tracks traffic and visit to member sites.

Niche Market: This is a narrowly defined segment with specific product features aimed at satisfying specific market needs, and demographics such as age, income, occupation, height, weight, religion, geographic area, and interest of the niche market.

NoFollow: An HTML attribute instructing search engines to not allow to hyperlink to a web page to be influenced in ranking by embedded links. The idea was implemented on website and emails to restrict certain types of searchengines spam.

Performance-Based Marketing: Marketing in which the merchant only pays commissions for results such as conversions to sales or leads.

Paid Placement: The method which a search engine provides space on its search engine result page to display links to a web site based on the highest bid for that space.

Podcast: An audio file downloaded from the web and play on demand using an Apple iPod or any MP3 media player

Platform: The place to launch software and application for third parties to offer additional applications to users. This includes some sort of hardware and software framework where the combination allows software, particularly application software to operate.

Profile: the online representation of a netizen's identity.

Public domain: A work enters the public domain when it is donated by its creator or when its copyright expires. A work in the public domain can be freely used in any way including commercial use.

RSS: (Really simple Syndication): A web standard for the delivery of content—blog entries, news stories, headlines, images, video— enabling readers to stay current with favorite publications or producers without having to browse from site to site. RSS feed let user subscribe to content automatically and read or listen to the material on computer or a portable device.

Search Engine Marketing (SEM): Also referred as Keyword Advertising, it is a form of internet marketing that uses short, text only ads, which are keyword based and appear when a potential customer enters a specific search phrase into a search engine.

Share: The act of sharing a piece of content with specific friends or "posting to profile" so that those friends particularly interested in it will read it.

Social Bookmarking: A method for Internet users to organize, store, manage and search for bookmarks of resources online.

Social Graph: an online representation of global mapping of real people to people network of relationships. This is created only through mutual consent

Social media: This includes web-based and mobile technologies used to for interactive communication and allow creation of digital content, audio text, or multimedia that are published and shared in a social environment, such as a blog, podcast, or forum.

Social media Optimization (SMO): A set of practice for generating publicity through social media, online communities and social networks. The focus is on driving traffic from sources other than search engines. SMO when implemented right, improves search ranking.

Social Network Service (SNS): An online environment to share, communicate and play with your friends through social networking sites.

Social news: Sometimes called social sites which encourage users to submit and vote on news stories or other links, thus determining which links are showcased.

Social tools: A software and platform that enable participatory culture. For example, blogs, podcasts, forums, wikis and shared videos and presentations.

Smartphone: It is a wireless mobile device that provides advanced computing functions in addition to making telephone calls. It can connects to the internet, sends and receives email, etc. It is able to run operating software and provides a platform for application developers.

Streaming media: Unlike downloadable products or videos, streaming media refers to video or audio that can be watched or listened to online but not stored permanently.

Syndication: Allows your blog content to be distributed online.

Tag cloud: Frequently used as website navigation aids, the terms are hyperlinked to items associated with the tag. Popular tags are often shown in a large type and less popular tags in smaller type.

Tagging: The act of allocating keywords to content created.

Tag: One or more keywords or phrases created by a blogger to help categorize each blog entry and make it easier to search and be found by web surfers and internet search engines.

Target Audience: This is the core audience of your blog or website.

Template: A pre-created design that can be customized into a blog, web page, website, or another piece of digital content. The popular blog hosting services offer dozens or in some cases hundreds of free blog templates you can use to create your blog so that it looks professional with full functionality and, without having to do any programming.

Traffic: Refers to the number of web surfers who visit your blog or website on an hourly, daily, weekly, monthly, or annual basis. A visitor is someone who surfs over to your blog or website.

Threads: Strands of conversation. On an email list or web forum they will be defined by messages that use the use the some subject. On blogs they are less clearly defined, but emerge through comments and trackback.

Tweet: A post on twitter, a real-time social messaging system.

URL (Uniform Resource Locators): This is a blog or website's address. A typical URL has three main components. The first part typically begins with "www" or "http://". The second part of a URL is what you actually must select. The third part of a URL is its extension, which is typically ".com", however, a variety of other extensions are available, such as .edu, .org, .net, .gov, .info, .TV, .biz, .name, and .us.

Videoblog (or vlog): A blog that contains video entries, some people call it video podcasting, vodcasting or vlogging.

Virtual World: An online simulated space that makes aspects of real life with fantasy elements.

Voice over Interenet Protocol: (VOIP): It enables you to use a computer or other internet device for phone calls without additional charges, including conference calls. Skype is one example.

Web Browser: The software that is used by web surfers to surf the web and access blogs. Microsoft Explorer, Safari, and FireFox are examples of popular web browsers.

Website Traffic: The amount of visitors and visits a Web site receives.

Webhosting Service: This is a type of Internet hosting service that allows individuals and organizations to make their own website accessible via the World Wide Web. Web hosts are companies that provide space on a server they own or lease for use by their clients as well as providing Internet connectivity. Web hosts can also provide data center space and online based tools to create, publish and manage the website.

Web 2.0: The second generation of the web, which enables people with no specialized technical knowledge to create their own website to self-publish. Create and upload audio and video files, share photos and information and complete a variety of other tasks.

Web analytics: The measurement, collection, analysis and reporting of internet data for the purpose of understanding who your visitors are and optimizing your web site.

Web-based tools: Google, Yahoo and host of other commercial organizations provide an increasing range of free or low-cost tools including e-mail, calendars, word processing, and spreadsheets that can be used on the web rather than your desktop.

Webcasting: The ability to use the web to deliver live or delayed versions of audio or video broadcast.

Webinar: Short for web-based seminar, a webinar is a presentation, lecture, workshop, or seminar that is transmitted over the web.

Widget: A software system for launching applets on the web, a desktop system or a mobile phone, usually displayed in a small box, with a specific purpose such as providing update on news, that is constantly updating itself (typically via RSS) widgets make it easy to add dynamic content to your site a blog.

Wiki: It is a website whose users can add, modify, or delete its content via a web browser using a rich-text editor. Wikis are typically powered by wiki software and are often created collaboratively, by multiple users. A technology designed to allow many people to edit a web page by providing a trail of edits and changes.

Word-of-mouth marketing: Sometimes called conversational marketing, is an umbrella term for customers who tell other people how much they like a business, product, service, or event. The process can be used to engage and energize customer.